CW01481074

Wills and Inheritance Protocol

Other titles available from Law Society Publishing:

Assessment of Mental Capacity (3rd edn)
The British Medical Association and the Law Society

Charities as Beneficiaries
The Law Society's Private Client Section and the Institute of Legacy Management

Elderly Client Handbook (4th edn)
General editors: Caroline Bielanska, Martin Terrell; consultant editor: Gordan Ashton

Inheritance Act Claims
Tracey Angus, Anna Clarke, Paul Hewitt and Penelope Reed

Lasting Powers of Attorney (2nd edn)
Craig Ward

Mental Capacity (2nd edn)
Nicola Greaney, Fenella Morris and Beverley Taylor

Mental Health Tribunals
Philip Fennell, Penny Letts and Jonathan Wilson

Probate Practitioner's Handbook (6th edn)
General editor: Lesley King

Trust Practitioner's Handbook (3rd edn)
Gill Steel

Will Draftsman's Handbook (9th edn)
Robin Riddett, Lesley King and Peter Gausden

Wills and Inheritance Quality Scheme Toolkit (forthcoming, 2013)
The Law Society

Titles from Law Society Publishing can be ordered from all good bookshops or direct (telephone 0870 850 1422, email **lawsociety@prolog.uk.com** or visit our online shop at **bookshop.lawsociety.org.uk**).

WILLS AND INHERITANCE PROTOCOL

The Law Society

The Law Society

Crown copyright material in Appendix A is reproduced with the permission of the Controller of Her Majesty's Stationery Office

ISBN-13: 978-1-907698-80-4

Published in 2013 by the Law Society
113 Chancery Lane, London WC2A 1PL

Typeset by Columns Design XML Ltd, Reading
Printed by TJ International Ltd, Padstow, Cornwall

The paper used for the text pages of this book is FSC® certified. FSC (the Forest Stewardship Council®) is an international network to promote responsible management of the world's forests.

FSC
www.fsc.org
MIX
Paper from
responsible sources
FSC® C013056

Contents

CONTENTS

Foreword

My own firm in Lancaster was started by a then sole practitioner in 1949. The world has changed significantly since Joseph A. Jones opened the doors of his new legal practice. One of his daughters is now our senior partner and she remembers him driving home for a leisurely lunch most days. The traffic in Lancaster would not permit such a luxury nowadays, never mind the telephone calls, emails and other demands which contemporary solicitors now deal with.

We cannot go back to the less hectic world of 1949, but one constant since then, at my firm and other solicitors' practices up and down the country, is the expertise and high level of service which we offer to our clients. These two attributes, which have been hallmarks of our profession for generations, are encapsulated in the new Law Society Wills and Inheritance Protocol.

This detailed and yet highly readable Protocol has been drafted by Lesley King with assistance from a Steering Group of volunteer practitioners drawn from the Law Society's Private Client Section Executive Committee and the Wills and Equity Committee. It is, I believe, the first time that preferred practice in wills, probate and estate administration has been brought together in a single document.

For practices accredited by the new Wills and Inheritance Quality Scheme (WIQS), adoption of the Protocol will be a mandatory requirement, but its use is also recommended to all members of the profession. I trust, however, that most solicitors reading this book will believe as I do, that the WIQS provides a unique opportunity to ensure that solicitors' practices remain the natural place to turn for clients seeking advice in this area of law.

This version of the Protocol is, I hope, likely to be the first of many in the future, as it is intended to be a living and dynamic document which will continue to evolve and improve in the future to reflect developments in the law and our profession.

Gary F. Rycroft, Chair of the WIQS Steering Group
Joseph A. Jones & Co Solicitors
Lancaster
August 2013

The Law Society Wills and Inheritance Protocol

ACKNOWLEDGEMENTS

The Law Society would like to thank Lesley King for her help with the drafting of this Protocol.

The Law Society would also like to thank the following members of the Wills and Inheritance Quality Scheme Steering Group for their scrutiny of the draft Protocol and their insightful suggestions for its improvement:

- Ian Bond
- Helen Clarke
- John Perry
- Gary Rycroft
- Patricia Wass
- Jonathan Smithers
- Richard Roberts
- Simon Leney.

The Law Society would like to thank past and present members of staff, including: Sarah Hunwick, Giselle Jauregui, Amy McCann and Maureen Miller for their valuable contributions.

For their support and expert review of the final draft, the Law Society would also like to thank:

- Bristol Law Society
- Cornwall Law Society
- Devon and Somerset Law Society
- Hertfordshire Law Society
- Institute of Legacy Management
- Kent Law Society
- Liverpool Law Society
- Members of the Law Society's Wills and Equity Committee
- Members of the Law Society's Private Client Section Executive Committee.

INTRODUCTION

The Law Society Wills and Inheritance Protocol (the Protocol) has been created to support the provision of *will drafting*, probate and *estate administration* services by its members. The impetus for creation of the Protocol has been the development of the Law Society's Wills and Inheritance Quality Scheme (WIQS).

The adoption of the Protocol, in so far as it is appropriate to the matter and in the best interests of the *client*, is mandatory for members of the WIQS and voluntary for all other members of the Law Society.

The Protocol aims to raise standards of client care and service by:

- setting out the Law Society's 'preferred practice' in *will drafting*, probate and *estate administration*;
- improving communication between *practices*, *clients* and beneficiaries;
- increasing transparency and therefore understanding of the *will drafting*, probate and *estate administration* processes; and
- encouraging *practices* to agree time frames and service levels with *clients*.

Adopting the Protocol will help a *practice* to:

- further distinguish itself from unregulated providers;
- demonstrate to *clients* and others its high standards of practice and client service;
- meet legal requirements;
- achieve and demonstrate compliance with its regulator's outcomes;
- provide a consistent high quality service; and
- recognise and reduce risks that may lead to negligence claims.

The Protocol contains general obligations, obligations specific to the provision of a particular service (**Parts A–E**); and obligations for a *practice* to have certain policies (**Parts F–H**).

The general obligations are, for the most part, designed to apply to provision of all the services covered by the Protocol, i.e. *will drafting*, probate and *estate administration*. As the Protocol and the WIQS intend to set standards in client service, the general obligations focus on this area and, where appropriate, draw upon existing standards and good practice.

The policies are intended to cover areas which are considered to commonly give rise to risks, errors and inconsistency in the course of providing *will drafting,* probate and *estate administration* services.

The Protocol does not prescribe the format and content of a policy in detail, but instead specifies certain points which must be addressed by a *practice* in a particular policy. A *practice* therefore has the flexibility to draft new policies or amend existing policies to deal with the requirements of the Protocol.

Carefully considered, regularly reviewed written policies which are communicated to all relevant partners and staff will help a *practice* to comply with legal and regulatory duties, achieve professional conduct outcomes and, if the *practice* is a member of the WIQS, to meet the Core Practice Management Standards.

No policy can cover every variable, so inevitably there will be cases where circumstances require the person providing the service to depart from the policy. However, a well considered policy will help the *practice* to anticipate problems, reduce risk and deliver a consistent, high quality service.

The Protocol will only reach its full potential if members of solicitors' practices share their experience of using it and their views on how it may be improved. Please direct any comments on the use and content of the Protocol to **wiqs@lawsociety.org.uk**.

DEFINED TERMS

Client includes potential client where the context admits.

Estate administration (also **administration of the estate**) means the process of transferring the assets of a deceased person to those entitled. Unless there is agreement to the contrary the process will normally include:
  (a) ascertaining the assets and liabilities of the deceased;
  (b) calculating taxes due;
  (c) obtaining a grant of representation;
  (d) collecting the assets of the deceased;
  (e) paying debts, taxes and administration expenses;
  (f) selling assets, if necessary, to realise cash for the purposes of the administration;
  (g) transferring the assets to those entitled;
  (h) producing estate accounts showing income and capital separately;
  (i) providing statements of income and income tax paid to beneficiaries with an income entitlement.

Guardian means a *guardian* (other than a *guardian* of the estate of a child) appointed in accordance with the provisions of the Children Act 1989, s.5.

Minor means a person aged under 18.

Parental responsibility has the meaning given to it in the Children Act 1989, s.3.

Practice means a *practice* authorised and regulated by the Solicitors Regulation Authority (SRA), including: any SRA authorised and regulated partnership, company, sole practitioner, limited liability partnership, legal disciplinary partnership, and alternative business structure which offers services to:
  (a) draft wills; or
  (b) obtain a grant of representation; or
  (c) deal with any aspect of *estate administration*.

Will drafter means the person preparing a will and, where the context permits, includes the person taking instructions for the will, if different.

Will drafting

means the process of ascertaining a *client's* wishes in relation to the assets that will pass on the *client's* death and the production of a will carrying out those wishes effectively.

Unless there is agreement to the contrary the process will normally include:

(a) obtaining information on the assets, liabilities, family and dependants of the *client*;

(b) advice on any lifetime steps necessary to allow the will to take effect, e.g. severance of a beneficial joint tenancy;

(c) an explanation of the way in which inheritance tax is likely to impact on the *client's* estate;

(d) a brief explanation of the fact that the Inheritance (Provision for Family and Dependants) Act 1975 allows certain family members and dependants to apply to the court if they consider that reasonable financial provision has not been made for them on death and a general consideration of whether the proposed dispositions of the estate might fail to make reasonable provision for potential applicants;

(e) advice on the correct execution of the will and, where the will is returned to the *will drafter* after execution, a check that the will appears to have been correctly executed; and

(f) advice on the need to review a will periodically and after significant life events and a warning, where appropriate, of the effects of marriage and divorce and the formation and dissolution of a *UK civil partnership*.

UK civil partnership

means a civil partnership within the meaning of the Civil Partnership Act 2004, s.1.

GENERAL OBLIGATIONS

Client communication

OB.1   Treat all *clients* with dignity and respect, in a manner which is sensitive to the circumstances.

OB.2   *Practices* which are members of the WIQS will give *clients* a copy of the WIQS Client Service Charter or direct the *client* to where the Charter can be viewed online.

OB.3   At the outset, give *clients* an explanation of the issues raised, the options for dealing with them, the processes involved, and a likely time frame for the matter.

OB.4   At the outset, give *clients* in writing the name and status of the person responsible for dealing with the matter and the name and status of the person responsible for the overall supervision of the matter.

OB.5   At the outset, agree an appropriate level of service with the *client*, including the means and frequency of communications.

OB.6   Respond promptly to *clients'* reasonable requests for information about the matter. *Practices* which are members of the WIQS will, unless otherwise agreed with the *client*:

    (a)   acknowledge all communications from *clients* within 48 hours of receipt; and

    (b)   if substantive points raised cannot be dealt with within that period, provide a time frame for doing so.

OB.7   Ensure that *clients* are informed as to the progress of the matter. *Practices* which are members of the WIQS will, unless otherwise agreed with the *client*, provide a progress report every 28 days when dealing with the *administration of an estate*.

OB.8   Carry out tasks in a timely manner.

OB.9   Where something is to be addressed by different means or a process is changed and this will directly affect the *client*, notify the *client* as soon as possible.

OB.10   If the person responsible for dealing with the matter or the person with responsibility for its overall supervision changes, inform the *client* in writing of the new person's name and status as soon as possible.

OB.11   Inform *clients* as soon as possible of any delays or changes to the time frame originally given and give a full explanation as to the nature of and reasons for any delay. This includes any delay caused by issues at the *practice*, e.g. illness of staff members.

OB.12   Communicate with *clients* in a form which is appropriate to their needs and circumstances.

OB.13   Communicate with *clients* in plain English using clear, understandable language, avoiding legal terminology unless necessary and, where it is used, providing sufficient explanation to allow *clients* to understand unfamiliar words and concepts.

Costs

OB.14   At the outset, give *clients* a clear explanation of the costs and how the *practice* charges for the service in question, including whether there will be a charge for an initial consultation.

OB.15   At the outset, give *clients* a clear explanation of any referral fee arrangements which could affect the *client's* matter.

OB.16   Explain in full how the *practice* charges for its services, whether it be by fixed costs, hourly rate or any other method of charging and, if unable to give an exact figure, give *clients* clear and realistic estimates of the likely costs.

OB.17   If the method of charging is changed, inform the *client* immediately and give an explanation as to why the charges have been changed.

OB.18   If it becomes evident during the course of the *client's* matter that the costs are likely to exceed the estimate originally given, inform the *client* immediately and give a breakdown of costs and an explanation of why they have increased.

Vulnerable clients

OB.19   Consider whether *clients* may be vulnerable, for example, due to disability, learning difficulties, mental health, infirmity and illness, age, bereavement and emotional distress.

OB.20   Be aware of the potential for financial abuse of *clients* and understand your role in both preventing it and taking action to protect *clients* who have been financially abused.

OB.21   Take particular care to ensure that vulnerable *clients* fully understand the services they require and that they are able to make informed decisions.

OB.22   Take particular care not to put any pressure on vulnerable *clients* when selling or promoting services.

Sales practices

OB.23   Ensure that publicity is fair and well balanced.

OB.24   Ensure that the *practice's* publicity material:

    (a)   does not make misleading claims as to the advantages that can be gained by making a will;

    (b)   does not advertise basic wills at a very low price with the intention that *clients* will then be pressured to buy more complex wills and further services which are not in their best interests;

    (c)   does not make unjustifiable or misleading statements about the skill and/or charging structures of other types of provider of legal services.

OB.25   Ensure that *clients* are not intimidated or pressured by the *practice* to give instructions for a service.

OB.26   Be pro-active in offering services which are in a *client's* best interests, explaining the benefits and risks so that the *client* can make an informed choice as to the services he/she requires.

OB.27   Ensure that publicity material complies with statutory requirements and that you have regard to voluntary codes and to the Law Society's Publicising Solicitors' Charges Practice Note.

Quality

OB.28   Only accept instructions from a *client* if the *practice* has suitable levels of expertise to deliver the service and ensure the quality of service.

OB.29   Ensure that:

    (a)   work is allocated to those who have the expertise to deal with it appropriately;

    (b)   there is a system of supervision in place which is robust enough to identify issues of quality; and

    (c)   there is a clear process requiring anyone who finds that work allocated to them is beyond their expertise to alert the person supervising them so that alternative arrangements can be made.

OB.30   Encourage *client* feedback by appropriate means, e.g. a short survey/feedback form.

OB.31   Have in place a system for reviewing feedback on a regular basis and identifying necessary modifications of processes.

Practice policies

OB.32   *Practices* will have the policies, set out in **Parts F**, **G** and **H** below, appropriate to the service provided to mitigate risks to the *client* and to the *practice*.

PART A

WILL DRAFTING

1 ARRANGEMENTS FOR TAKING INSTRUCTIONS

1.1 Identify and deal appropriately with visual, communication and mobility problems in accordance with the *practice's* policy for *clients* with a disability (see **GP.1** in **Part F** below).

1.2 To help avoid any later suggestion of undue influence, explain to the *client* why it is preferable to take instructions in the absence of potential beneficiaries and persons who may exert undue influence. If the *client* chooses to have such a person with him/her, record the advice given and the *client's* response and preserve as part of the will file.

1.3 When taking instructions from the *client* with another person present, be alert to the possibility of undue influence and the added difficulty of assessing mental capacity when another person provides information. Do not continue to act if there is evidence that the *client* is subject to undue influence.

1.4 Where language and/or disability make it impossible to communicate directly with the *client*, arrange for an interpreter or person trained in communication skills to attend the interview so that instructions can be taken independently of a potential beneficiary.

1.5 Joint instructions

1.5.1 If married couples, or civil partners, or cohabitees, or close friends wish to attend the interview together to give joint instructions for their wills, at or before the interview:

    (a) check that each *client* is willing to give instructions in the presence of the other, given that sensitive matters have to be discussed, record the enquiry and *client's* response and preserve as part of the will file;

    (b) explain to each *client* that if a conflict of interests arises the *will* *drafter* will not be able to continue to act for both (or all) *clients* and may have to cease acting for all *clients*;

(c) explain to each *client* that the *will drafter* will not accept instructions to make subsequent significant changes to the will of one *client* without the knowledge of the other *client(s)* (unless the other lacks mental capacity).

1.6 Earlier wills

1.6.1 Ascertain whether the *practice* has made an earlier will for the *client* and, if so, retrieve the will file from storage and read the earlier will.

1.6.2 If the *client* has made an earlier will which is not stored by the *practice*, ask the *client* to bring the earlier will, or a copy, if the original is not available.

1.6.3 Where another *practice* has prepared an earlier will for the *client* and is storing the original will, ask for the *client's* permission to request that the other *practice* supplies the original earlier will.

1.6.4 Discuss with the *client* the reasons for changes from any earlier wills.

1.7 Contracts made 'off premises'

1.7.1 Where a contract for the drafting of a will is made:

(a) during a visit to the *client's* home or home of another person or workplace; or

(b) during a visit to a hospital or residential home where the *client* is staying; or

(c) during an excursion organised by the *practice*; or

(d) after an offer made by the *client* during such a visit or excursion;

comply with the Cancellation of Contracts made in a Consumer's Home or Place of Work etc. Regulations 2008 (the Regulations).

1.7.2 To comply with the Regulations the person selling the service:

(a) must give to the *client* a written notice of the *client's* right to cancel the contract within seven days;

(b) where, as will usually be the case with *will drafting* instructions, a delay of seven days is not in the *client's* best interests, ask the *client* to provide written instructions to start work within the cooling-off period;

(c) explain to the *client* that the contract can be cancelled before the end of the cancellation period even though work has commenced, but the *client* may have to pay for any work that was carried out on his/her behalf before cancellation in accordance with the reasonable requirements of the agreement.

1.7.3 Where a visit or excursion follows the making of a contract, be aware that the Regulations will apply if the contract is subsequently varied during such a visit or excursion.

Notes:

(i) Cancellation of Contracts made in a Consumer's Home or Place of Work etc. Regulations 2008 (SI 2008/1816).

(ii) See the Law Society's Cancellation of Contracts Practice Note.

2 TAKING INSTRUCTIONS

2.1 Urgent instructions

2.1.1 Inevitably some wills have to be prepared as a matter of urgency, for example, where a *client* is nearing death or wishes to make a will very quickly. In such cases the *will drafter* should:

(a) comply with the *practice's* policy on urgent instructions (see **WP.4** in **Part G** below); and

(b) decide whether it is in the best interests of the *client* to ignore certain obligations of the Protocol in order to produce a will within the required time frame.

2.1.2 The *will drafter* must:

(a) assess the *client's* capacity to give instructions as set out at obligation **2.7** below;

(b) check that the *client* is not subject to undue influence; and

(c) produce a will that effectively carries out the *client's* testamentary wishes.

2.2 Attendance notes

2.2.1 Use a template document to record notes of the interview in accordance with the *practice's* policy on attendance notes (see **WP.6** in **Part G** below).

2.2.2 In the attendance note, make a detailed and contemporaneous record of:

(a) the domicile of the *client* and any spouse or civil partner;

(b) the assets of the *client* including those which do not pass by will;

(c) the liabilities of the *client* and whether these are secured;

(d) the names of the *client's* family and dependants;

(e) any advice given;

(f) the *client's* testamentary wishes;

(g) the *will drafter's* assessment of the *client's* testamentary capacity, the questions asked to establish it and the *client's* responses;

(h) whether there was anything to suggest possible undue influence; and

wherever appropriate, record the actual words used by the *client*.

2.2.3 In the case of elderly or ill *clients* where, although it appears there may be time to prepare a draft, a sudden loss of capacity is possible, consider whether it is prudent to ask the *client* to sign the attendance note to indicate that it is an accurate record of what was agreed at the interview.

2.2.4 Preserve the attendance note as part of the will file. In the event of a dispute as to the validity of the will, it will be important evidence.

2.2.5 Retain the will file for an appropriate period in accordance with the *practice's* policy on storage of wills and retention of files (see **WP.8** in **Part G** below). This will normally be at least until a grant of representation is obtained to the *client's* estate. In some instances it may be appropriate to retain the will file for some time afterwards in case of future litigation.

2.2.6 If the *practice* has appropriate facilities, consider making a video recording of the interview. If this is done, refer to the recording in the attendance note and ensure that the recording is retained for viewing in future.

2.3 Non-face-to-face instructions

2.3.1 In accordance with the *practice's* policy on taking instructions (see **WP.1** in **Part G** below) where the *practice* takes instructions without a face-to-face interview, preserve and retain:

(a) the preliminary information provided to *clients*;

(b) any checklist or information sheet completed by *clients*; and

(c) the instructions for the will prepared;

for the same period as attendance notes of face-to-face meetings.

2.4 Time limits for the preparation of the will

2.4.1 At the time when instructions are received from the *client*, agree a date for the preparation of the will which:

(a) is acceptable to the *client*; and

(b) reflects any need for urgency.

2.4.2   Unless otherwise agreed, once the *client* has provided all the information required to complete the agreed instructions:

(a)   send the draft will to the *client* within seven working days; and

(b)   send the final version to the *client* for execution within seven working days of receiving approval of the draft; or

(c)   if a draft is not supplied, send the will to the *client* for execution within 10 working days.

2.4.3   If a draft will or letter requesting instructions has been sent but the *client* does not respond, comply with obligation **15** below.

2.5   Gathering information

2.5.1   Ask the *client* to give an outline of his/her assets, liabilities, family and dependants and priorities in relation to the disposition of the estate.

2.5.2   Use follow-up questions to establish any matters in relation to property which will affect the terms of the will, including but not limited to:

(a)   whether any assets are co-owned and, if so, whether such assets are held as beneficial joint tenants or tenants in common;

(b)   whether any third parties may have interests in property apparently owned by the *client* through either constructive or resulting trusts or assurances made by the *client* which might give rise to a claim for proprietary estoppel;

(c)   whether the *client* may have interests in property apparently owned by third parties through such trusts or assurances;

(d)   details of any death in service benefits, the terms of such benefits and any nomination already made by the *client*;

(e)   details of any life assurance policies, the terms of such policies, and any assignments or declarations of trust already made by the *client*;

(f)   details of any funeral or lifetime care plans taken out by the *client*;

(g)   whether the *client* has any interest under a settlement, is a trustee or has a power of appointment over trust assets;

(h)   whether the *client* owns or has an interest in a business;

(i)   whether the *client* has any foreign property and, if so, whether any advice has been obtained as to the local inheritance laws;

(j)   whether the *client* expects to inherit property;

(k)   whether the *client* has made any lifetime transfers of value; and

(l)   what liabilities the *client* has and whether any are secured.

2.5.3   In a case where information about assets is held by third parties, such as financial advisers and accountants, seek the *client's* consent to obtain necessary information from those third parties and retain it.

2.5.4 Use follow-up questions to prepare a list of dependants and family members including any cohabitee.

2.5.5 Establish the *client's* testamentary wishes and consider whether any specific advice is required in light of the information gathered.

2.6 Personal assets log

2.6.1 Suggest that, to facilitate the *administration of the estate*, the *client*:

(a) completes and maintains a list of assets, including digital assets; and

(b) considers how to ensure that those dealing with the estate will be able to access those assets.

2.6.2 Recommend that the *client* completes the Law Society's Personal Assets Log, or similar document, for this purpose.

2.7 Ascertaining testamentary capacity

2.7.1 *Will drafters* must be aware of the implications of the series of cases, starting with *Kenward* v. *Adams*, which set out good practice in circumstances where there may be later questions as to testamentary capacity. These implications are summarised below.

In *Kenward* v. *Adams*, Templeman J stated that:

> ... in the case of an aged testator or a testator who has suffered a serious illness, there is one golden rule which should always be observed, however straightforward matters may appear, and however difficult or tactless it may be to suggest that precautions be taken. The making of a will by such a testator ought to be witnessed or approved by a medical practitioner who satisfies himself of the capacity and understanding of the testator, and records and preserves his examination and findings.

The so-called 'golden rule' is not a rule of law, it is merely a statement of good practice. Failure to obtain a medical opinion does not invalidate the will. It simply means that there is no contemporaneous medical evidence to assist the court in a dispute as to testamentary capacity.

It is not always possible to obtain a medical opinion as:

(a) the *client* may be unwilling to consent to such an examination; or

(b) it may be impossible or impracticable to obtain such an opinion within the necessary time frame; or

(c) the *client's* capacity is likely to deteriorate quickly; or

(d) death is imminent.

15

2.7.2   If it is not possible for the *will drafter* to obtain a medical opinion on the testamentary capacity of the *client* in accordance with the 'golden rule':

(a)   explain to the *client* that, in the event of a subsequent challenge to the will on the basis of lack of capacity, the lack of a contemporaneous medical opinion may make the challenge more likely to succeed; and

(b)   ask the *client* to confirm that they wish to continue, record the advice given and the *client's* decision, and preserve as part of the will file.

2.7.3   Whenever proceeding without a medical opinion:

(a)   Ask the *client* open questions to establish whether, on the balance of probabilities, the *client* fulfills the test of testamentary capacity as set out in *Banks* v. *Goodfellow*. According to this test, the *client* should:

(i)   understand the nature of the will-making act and its effects;

(ii)   understand the extent of the property of which the *client* is disposing;

(iii)   comprehend and appreciate the claims to which the *client* ought to give effect; and

(iv)   not suffer from any disorder of the mind or delusion that prevents rational consideration of these matters and produces a disposition which the *client* would not otherwise have made.

(b)   Try to establish whether the *client* can:

(i)   retain the information relevant to decisions as to the disposition of the estate throughout the decision-making process;

(ii)   use or weigh that information as part of the process of making the decisions; and

(iii)   communicate these decisions.

(c)   Record the questions asked and the replies of the *client* together with your assessment of the *client's* testamentary capacity and preserve as part of the will file.

2.7.4   If satisfied that the *client* has sufficient testamentary capacity to make the will in question, proceed to prepare the will.

2.7.5   If satisfied that the *client* does not have sufficient testamentary capacity to make the will in question:

(a)   consider whether the *client's* testamentary capacity may fluctuate so that it might be possible to take instructions at a later date and, if so, arrange a further appointment;

(b)   consider the likelihood that seeing the *client* at a different time of day and/or in a different environment, e.g. at home, may improve the *client's* testamentary capacity;

(c) where it appears unlikely that the *client* will recover capacity, have regard to the guidance in the Law Society's Financial Abuse Practice Note; and

(d) prepare and preserve as part of the will file the attendance note setting out the reasons for determining that the *client* lacked testamentary capacity.

2.7.6 If uncertain whether the *client* has testamentary capacity, consider whether it may still be in the *client's* best interests to make the will. It will be particularly important to:

(a) explain the situation to the *client*;

(b) obtain confirmation that the *client* wishes to proceed; and

(c) prepare and preserve as part of the will file the attendance note setting out the reasons for uncertainty as to the *client's* testamentary capacity and the reasons for continuing to make the will.

2.7.7 Where it appears that the *client's* capacity fluctuates, consider whether the *client* may also want advice on how to plan for times when they do not have mental capacity.

2.7.8 If obtaining a medical opinion as to testamentary capacity:

(a) instruct a medical practitioner with appropriate expertise in the assessment of capacity;

(b) provide clear written guidance for the medical practitioner on the legal test of testamentary capacity;

(c) with the *client's* consent, give the medical practitioner a summary of the complexity of the *client's* affairs and the proposed dispositions of the estate;

(d) ensure that the assessment is as close as possible to the time when instructions are given and the will is executed (as mental capacity can fluctuate); and

(e) if possible, the medical practitioner should be present at execution even if, as is often the case, professional regulations prevent them acting as a witness.

Notes:

(i)   *Kenward* v. *Adams* [1975] CLY 3591.

(ii)   *Banks* v. *Goodfellow* (1870) LR 5 QB 549.

(iii)   For further guidance and a sample letter to a medical practitioner requesting an assessment of testamentary capacity, see *Assessment of Mental Capacity: A practical guide for doctors and lawyers* 3rd edition (Law Society, 2010).

(iv)   See the Law Society's Financial Abuse Practice Note.

2.8   Potential for financial abuse

2.8.1   When taking instructions, the *will drafter* should be alert to signs of potential financial abuse, particularly in the following instances:

(a)   Where the person making the will is not being allowed individual access to the *will drafter*.

(b)   Where instructions come from a third party.

(c)   Where instructions are coming from a third party who is to benefit from the will.

(d)   Where a third party is always present at an interview with the *will drafter*.

(e)   Where a third party is using their own solicitor to prepare a will for a vulnerable person who has previously had his/her own solicitor.

Note:

(i)   See the Law Society's Financial Abuse Practice Note.

2.9   Consideration of earlier wills

2.9.1   If earlier wills are available (see obligation **1.6** above), consider whether they highlight issues which need to be dealt with, such as those in **(a)–(d)** below:

(a)   *The existence of foreign property*

(i)   Ascertain what, if any, arrangements are in place in relation to the disposition of the foreign property.

(ii)   Consider whether the new will should be limited to assets in England and Wales.

(iii)   Consider whether the new will should limit the revocation clause to wills dealing with property in England and Wales.

(b)   *A settled pattern of testamentary dispositions from which the client is departing*

Try to ascertain the reasons for the change to exclude the possibility of undue influence or doubtful testamentary capacity.

(c) ***Property or relatives not mentioned by the client***
Ascertain whether circumstances have changed or whether the *client* has forgotten property or persons, casting doubt on the *client's* testamentary capacity.

(d) ***A mutual wills agreement reciting that the will cannot be unilaterally revoked***
Establish whether the other party to the agreement is still alive and advise appropriately.

3 ADVICE ON ASSETS PASSING INDEPENDENTLY OF THE WILL

3.1 Standard advice to be provided as part of the will drafting retainer

3.1.1 Establish whether the *client* has any property which cannot pass under the terms of a will, for example:

(a) an interest held as a beneficial joint tenant;
(b) the proceeds of a life assurance policy which, before death, have been assigned to, or written in trust for, another person;
(c) nominated death in service benefits; and
(d) property passing under the terms of a settlement.

3.1.2 Explain to the *client* how such property will pass on death.

3.1.3 Establish whether the proposed disposition of the estate is in accordance with the *client's* wishes once the assets passing independently of the will are taken into account. If it is not, advise the *client* that:

(a) the proposed testamentary dispositions can be adjusted; and
(b) steps can be taken before death to change the terms on which the assets passing independently of the will are held, for example by severing a beneficial joint tenancy.

3.1.4 Establish whether the *client* wishes to receive detailed advice on the steps to change the terms on which assets passing independently of the will are held.

3.1.5 If the *practice* has the necessary expertise to provide such advice, ensure that the charge for this work is made clear to the *client* before any action is taken.

3.1.6 If the *practice* does not have the necessary expertise, suggest that the *client* takes separate advice and, if the *practice* has relevant knowledge, assist the *client* to identify a suitable adviser, but consider whether it is in the *client's* best interests for the *practice* to cease to act in relation to the preparation of the will.

3.2 Further advice and action which a client may require on property held as beneficial joint tenants

3.2.1 If the *client's* testamentary wishes cannot be achieved without severance, offer to implement severance.

3.2.2 Where a *client* is uncertain as to whether assets are owned as beneficial joint tenants or tenants in common, offer to assist the *client* to establish the basis of ownership and offer to draft and serve a precautionary notice of severance.

3.2.3 Check whether the *practice's will drafting* retainer excludes the preparation of ancillary documentation and advise the *client* of any separate charge for this work.

3.3 Further advice and action which a client may require on life assurance

3.3.1 If appropriate, advise the *client* that:

(a) life assurance policies which have already been written in trust or assigned are no longer in the beneficial ownership of the *client* and his/her disposition cannot be altered, so the *client* must take the disposition into account when determining the terms of the will; and

(b) in unusual cases, a revocable assignment or declaration can be made, in which case further assignments or declarations are possible.

3.3.2 If life assurance is still in the beneficial ownership of the *client*, discuss with the *client* whether it is in his/her best interests to:

(a) assign the policy to another person; or

(b) declare that it is held on trust for another person.

3.3.3 The *practice* should offer to prepare the necessary documentation if it has the expertise necessary to do so.

3.3.4 If the *practice* does not have the necessary expertise, suggest that the *client* takes separate advice and, if the *practice* has relevant knowledge, assist the *client* to identify a suitable adviser, but consider whether it is in the *client's* best interests for the *practice* to cease to act in relation to the preparation of the will.

3.3.5   Check whether the *practice's will drafting* retainer excludes the preparation of ancillary documentation and advise the *client* of any separate charge
for this work.

3.3.6   If instructed to prepare such documentation, carry out customer due
diligence if not already completed.

3.4   Further advice and action which a client may require on death in service benefits

3.4.1   If the terms of the death in service scheme allow employees to nominate
who they wish to receive lump sums payable on death, advise the *client* of:

(a)   the importance of making a nomination;

(b)   the importance of making nominations that are appropriate in light of
the terms of the will; and

(c)   the straightforward nature of the documents the *client* can use to
make a nomination.

3.4.2   If the *client* gives specific instructions to prepare the nomination document,
check whether the *practice's will drafting* retainer excludes the preparation
of ancillary documentation and ensure that the charge for this work, if any,
is made clear to the *client* before any action is taken.

3.5   Further advice and action which a client may require on property passing under the terms of a settlement

3.5.1   Where a *client* is a life tenant or a remainderman of a fixed settlement,
advise the *client* that it may be possible to achieve a more beneficial result
if:

(a)   the interest is assigned or surrendered; or

(b)   the whole trust is brought to an end by agreement between the various
beneficiaries.

3.5.2   If instructed, explore the possibility of such action and, where appropriate,
take the necessary steps.

3.5.3   Carry out customer due diligence if not already completed.

3.5.4   Where a *client* is a member of a class of beneficiaries of a discretionary
settlement, consider whether it is appropriate to provide the trustees with
information as to the circumstances of the *client*.

3.5.5   If instructed, write to the trustees providing the relevant information.

3.5.6   If instructed to deal with trust interests, ensure that the charge for this work is made clear to the *client* before any action is taken.

4   ADVICE ON THIRD PARTY RIGHTS

4.1   Standard advice on third party rights to be provided as part of the will drafting retainer

4.1.1   If the *client* owns property with another person, check whether the beneficial ownership is clear. If it is not, advise the *client* that because disputes after death can be difficult and expensive to settle, it is preferable to take steps to clarify the position before death.

4.1.2   If it becomes apparent that the *client* and a third party may have interests under a constructive or resulting trust, or an entitlement to assets arising from proprietary estoppel, explain to the *client*:

(a)   that such interests may exist; and

(b)   in general terms, how these interests would affect the *client's* estate on death.

4.1.3   Establish whether or not the *client* wishes to receive detailed advice on identifying, recording or changing beneficial interests.

4.1.4   If the *practice* has the expertise necessary to provide such advice, ensure that the charge for this work is made clear to the *client* before any action is taken.

4.1.5   If the *practice* does not have the necessary expertise, suggest that the *client* takes separate advice and, if the *practice* has relevant knowledge, assist the *client* to identify a suitable adviser, but consider whether it is in the *client's* best interests for the *practice* to cease to act in relation to the preparation of the will.

4.2   Further advice and action which a client may require on third party rights

4.2.1   Where it appears that problems in relation to third party interests may exist, explore with the *client* the extent to which the position can be clarified immediately.

4.2.2   If instructed, take such steps as are required to clarify the position.

4.2.3   Carry out customer due diligence if not already completed.

5   **ADVICE ON INHERITANCE (PROVISION FOR FAMILY AND DEPENDANTS) ACT 1975**

5.1   **Standard advice to be provided as part of the will drafting retainer**

5.1.1   Provide the *client* with:

   (a)   an outline of the effect of the Inheritance (Provision for Family and Dependants) Act 1975 (the Act);
   (b)   a summary of the potential applicants; and
   (c)   a warning if the *client's* instructions might give rise to an application under the Act.

5.1.2   Establish whether the *client* wishes to receive detailed advice on:

   (a)   the implications of the Act; and
   (b)   any steps which can be taken to minimise the chances of an application being successful.

5.1.3   If the *practice* has the expertise necessary to provide such detailed advice, make clear the charge that will be made before any action is taken.

5.1.4   If the *practice* does not have the necessary expertise, suggest that the *client* takes separate advice and, if the *practice* has relevant knowledge, assist the *client* to identify a suitable adviser, but consider whether it is in the *client's* best interests for the *practice* to cease to act in relation to the preparation of the will.

6   **ADVICE ON INHERITANCE TAX**

6.1   **Standard advice on inheritance tax to be provided as part of the will drafting retainer**

6.1.1   Advise the *client* whether, on the basis of current assets and liabilities, the disposition of the estate is likely to produce an inheritance tax liability. Such advice would normally include an explanation of:

   (a)   the likely amount of tax payable on the estate as a whole; and
   (b)   where the burden of tax will fall unless the will provides otherwise.

6.1.2   Establish whether the *client* wishes to change the disposition of the estate in light of that advice.

6.1.3   Draft the will appropriately, taking care to structure the dispositions in the will in the most tax efficient manner, if this is in accordance with the *client's* instructions.

6.1.4   Establish whether the *client* wishes to receive advice on mitigation of inheritance tax and/or other tax liabilities by lifetime planning.

6.1.5   If the *practice* has the expertise necessary to provide such advice, ensure that the charge for this work is made clear to the *client* before any action is taken.

6.1.6   If the *practice* does not have the necessary expertise, suggest that the *client* takes separate advice and, if the *practice* has relevant knowledge, assist the *client* to identify a suitable adviser, but consider whether it is in the *client's* best interests for the *practice* to cease to act in relation to the preparation of the will.

6.2   Further advice and action which a client may require on inheritance tax

6.2.1   If providing such advice, carry out customer due diligence if not already completed.

7   ADVICE ON FOREIGN PROPERTY

7.1   Unless the *practice* has the necessary expertise, explain to the *client* that:

    (a)   the *practice* cannot give advice on the succession of foreign property; and

    (b)   the situation of the property may prevent it from devolving under the will.

7.2   Recommend that the *client* seeks appropriate advice from a local expert.

7.3   If the *practice* has relevant knowledge, help the *client* to identify a suitable person.

7.4   If instructed to do so, provide the *client* with a letter to be given to the local expert explaining that there is an existing will which deals with the *client's* UK assets and that any local will should be limited to local assets and should not include a general revocation clause.

8   ADVICE ON BUSINESS AND AGRICULTURAL ASSETS

8.1   Standard advice on business and agricultural assets to be provided as part of the will drafting retainer

8.1.1   Advise the *client* that these assets may attract relief from inheritance tax but lifetime planning may have to be undertaken to maximise relief.

8.1.2   Where the *client* is a partner in a business, advise that partnership agreements normally contain provisions dealing with the death of a partner which need to be examined to ascertain their suitability.

8.1.3   Where the *client* holds shares in a limited company, advise that shares are often subject to pre-emption rights which, unless altered during the *client's* lifetime, may prevent the *client* from disposing of the shares freely.

8.1.4   Where the *client* is the sole owner of an unincorporated or incorporated business, advise the *client* to consider how the business will function after death and what succession planning can be put in place.

8.1.5   Establish whether the *client* wishes to receive detailed advice on dealing with the business or agricultural assets.

8.1.6   If the *practice* has the expertise necessary to offer such advice, ensure that the charge for this work is made clear to the *client* before any action is taken.

8.1.7   If the *practice* does not have the necessary expertise, suggest that the *client* takes separate advice and, if the *practice* has relevant knowledge, assist the *client* to identify a suitable adviser, but consider whether it is in the *client's* best interests for the *practice* to cease to act in relation to the preparation of the will.

8.2   Further advice and action which may be required where the client is a partner

8.2.1   Establish the terms of the partnership agreement in relation to the death of a partner.

8.2.2   Point out any ambiguity or unsatisfactory provisions in those terms, for example, the basis of valuation of the partnership assets.

8.2.3   Establish whether the *client* wants any further advice on the effect of the partnership agreement and possible amendments to it.

8.2.4   If the *client* does not want further advice, draft the will appropriately.

8.2.5   If the *client* does want further advice, and the *practice* has the expertise necessary to provide it, ensure that the charge for this work is made clear to the *client* before any action is taken.

8.2.6   If instructed to act, carry out customer due diligence if not already completed.

8.2.7   If the *practice* does not have the necessary expertise, suggest that the *client* obtains separate advice and, if the *practice* has relevant knowledge, assist the *client* to identify a suitable adviser, but consider whether in the best interests of the *client* the *practice* should cease to act in relation to the preparation of the will.

8.3   Further advice and action which may be required where the client is the sole owner of an unincorporated business

8.3.1   Establish whether the *client* has any plans for succession.

8.3.2   If the *client* does not have any plans for succession, point out that difficulties will arise if the *client* dies with no one able to deal with the day-to-day running of the business.

8.3.3   If there is someone with knowledge of the day-to-day running of the business:

(a)   discuss with the *client* the possible appointment of that person as a limited executor of the business;

(b)   discuss with the *client* the powers that person should have; and

(c)   if instructed, draft such an appointment appropriately, making clear any additional charge for this work.

8.3.4   The *client* may decide that incorporation or creation of a partnership is appropriate. If the *practice* has the expertise necessary to provide advice on the formation of such structures, ensure that the charge for this work is made clear to the *client* before any action is taken.

8.3.5   If instructed to act, carry out customer due diligence if not already completed.

8.3.6   If the *practice* does not have the necessary expertise, suggest that the *client* obtains separate advice and, if the *practice* has relevant knowledge, assist the *client* to identify a suitable adviser, but consider whether in the best interests of the *client* the *practice* should cease to act in relation to the preparation of the will.

8.4 **Further advice and action which may be required where the client runs a business through a limited liability company**

8.4.1 Establish whether there are other shareholders and directors or whether it is a 'one person' business, and:

(a) if it is a 'one person' business, consider the points raised at obligations **8.3.1–8.3.3** above with the *client*;

(b) if there are others involved in the business who will be able to continue the business after the death of the *client*, consider with the client the disposition of the shares.

8.4.2 Establish whether there are any pre-emption rights. If there are, discuss with the *client* whether the proposed disposition is satisfactory in light of those rights.

8.4.3 If the disposition is not satisfactory, consider with the *client* whether the pre-emption rights can be varied or whether alternative dispositions should be made.

8.4.4 The *client* may decide that variation of the pre-emption rights is appropriate. If the *practice* has the expertise necessary to provide advice, ensure that the charge for this work is made clear to the *client* before any action is taken.

8.4.5 If instructed to act, carry out customer due diligence if not already completed.

8.4.6 If the *practice* does not have the necessary expertise, suggest that the *client* obtains separate advice and, if the *practice* has relevant knowledge, assist the *client* to identify a suitable adviser, but consider whether in the best interests of the *client* the *practice* should cease to act in relation to the preparation of the will.

8.5 **Further advice and action which a client may require on inheritance tax and business assets**

8.5.1 Explain to a *client* with business assets, including agricultural assets, that they are likely to require specialist advice on the impact of inheritance tax and the possible availability of business and/or agricultural property relief.

8.5.2 If the *practice* has the expertise necessary, offer to provide advice, and ensure that the charge for this work is made clear to the *client* before any action is taken.

8.5.3 If so instructed, carry out customer due diligence if not already completed.

8.5.4 If the *practice* does not have the necessary expertise, suggest that the *client* obtains separate advice and, if the *practice* has relevant knowledge, assist the *client* to identify a suitable adviser, but consider whether in the best interests of the *client* the *practice* should cease to act in relation to the preparation of the will.

9 ADVICE ON THE NEED TO REVIEW THE WILL

9.1 Advise all *clients* that they should review their will every few years and always after there is a significant event such as a death, birth or decision to form or end a marriage or *UK civil partnership*.

9.2 Advise all *clients* that they should keep their Personal Assets Log (or other similar record of assets) up-to-date.

9.3 Advise single *clients* that marriage or the formation of a *UK civil partnership* revokes a will unless the will is made in expectation of marriage to, or formation of a *UK civil partnership* with, a particular person and includes a statement that it is not to be revoked by the marriage or formation of the *UK civil partnership*.

9.4 Advise *clients* who are married or in a *UK civil partnership* that the final decree of divorce or dissolution will:

(a) revoke gifts to the former spouse or civil partner; and

(b) revoke the appointment of the former spouse or civil partner as an executor.

10 PLANNING THE DISPOSITION OF THE ESTATE

10.1 General considerations

10.1.1 The *will drafter* should be aware that *clients* are often uncertain how best to achieve a satisfactory distribution of their assets, particularly where there are competing demands from second families. They will usually be unaware of the options available and of the effect of implied legal rules.

10.1.2 The *will drafter* should help the *client* to achieve his/her testamentary wishes in the most effective way.

10.1.3 Whenever advice is given to a *client* on alternative dispositions:

(a) provide the *client* with a written record of the advice; and

(b) preserve a copy of the record as part of the will file.

10.2   More effective ways to achieve the client's wishes

10.2.1   Explain the legal consequences of the *client's* instructions and any alternative ways in which the *client* may achieve a similar result more effectively.

10.3   Other action

10.3.1   Consider whether it is in the *client's* best interests for the practice to offer and discuss other related services such as lifetime gifts, creation of lifetime settlements, the making of a lasting power of attorney, prenuptial agreements and living together agreements.

10.4   Use of trusts

10.4.1   Where appropriate, explain the ways in which a trust can be used to:

(a)   protect capital; and

(b)   provide for different classes of beneficiary.

10.4.2   Explain the different types of trusts available and their respective advantages and disadvantages.

10.4.3   Advise on the importance of selecting appropriate trustees and the likely costs of administration.

10.5   Mutual wills agreements

10.5.1   *Will drafters* should be aware that it is normally preferable to use a formal trust structure rather than entering into a mutual wills agreement. However, there may be cases, particularly in relation to modest estates, where the use of such an agreement is justifiable.

10.5.2   Where the use of a mutual wills agreement is contemplated, provide a written explanation of the effect of the agreement, dealing with the following matters in particular:

(a)   The parties agree to leave specified assets in a particular way (normally to the other and, if the other has predeceased, to an agreed third party) and agree that they will not change the disposition of those assets without the consent of the other party.

(b)   Once the first party dies, the survivor is not free to change the disposition of the agreed assets in any way, so any will which purports to do so will be ineffective. On the second death the agreed assets will be held on trust for the third party.

(c)   During the survivor's lifetime the survivor is free to deal with those assets for his/her own benefit and may, for example, sell the assets and spend the proceeds on his/her own needs. There is no guarantee, therefore, that the third party will receive anything under the terms of the agreement.

(d) The survivor is not, however, free to give away or settle the agreed assets during his/her lifetime and any attempt to do so will result in a trust in favour of the agreed third party crystallising at that point.

(e) Advice that mutual will agreements carry the following inherent risks:

(i) there may be arguments over the existence of a binding agreement, its exact terms and the extent of the assets bound;

(ii) unless the agreed third party is aware of the existence of the agreement and has a written record of its existence and terms, the survivor may conceal the existence of the agreement and make a new will in contravention of the terms of the agreement, which goes unchallenged.

10.5.3 If the *clients* agree that they want their wills to be mutual:

(a) agree on the assets which are to be subject to the agreement;

(b) include a clear recital in the will of the agreement and its terms;

(c) prepare a separate agreement that sets out the terms and is signed by both parties (this is essential if the agreement relates to land but desirable in all cases for the avoidance of doubt); and

(d) give each party a copy of the agreement and discuss the desirability of providing the agreed third party or parties with a copy.

10.5.4 If the *clients* decide after discussion that they do not want the wills to be mutual, record this agreement in writing and include a statement to that effect in each will to avoid subsequent argument and uncertainty.

10.6 Provision for pets

10.6.1 *Clients* are often concerned to make provision for the care of pets after their death. Explain the options and their relative merits, such as:

(a) give the animal and a cash sum to the executors with a request that they deal with both in accordance with an expression of wishes; or

(b) give the animal and a cash sum to a named individual with a proviso that the legatee must undertake to care for the animal, and a gift over to another beneficiary in default of the undertaking; or

(c) give the animal and a cash sum to an appropriate animal charity with a direction that the charity finds the animal a suitable home; or

(d)   create a trust limited to 21 years leaving funds to trustees to be used for the care of the animal with a gift over.

11   THE TERMS OF THE WILL

11.1   Recording advice and decisions

11.1.1   The detailed contents of the will require the *client* to make a number of decisions. Provide the *client* with a written record of the decisions made and of the advice on which these decisions were made, and preserve a copy as part of the will file.

11.2   Client's wishes for funeral arrangements and organ donation

11.2.1   Establish the *client's* wishes, if any, with regard to funeral arrangements and organ donation.

11.2.2   Consider whether it is appropriate to encourage the *client* to make any wishes for funeral arrangements known to those who will be dealing with them.

11.2.3   Consider whether it is appropriate to encourage the *client* to make lifetime arrangements for organ donation.

11.2.4   If the *client* instructs, include appropriate statements of wishes in the will.

11.3   Subsequent marriage or formation of civil partnership

11.3.1   In the case of a single *client* in a close relationship, advise the *client* on the option to include a statement in the will that the will is made in expectation of marriage or the formation of a *UK civil partnership* to the named individual.

11.3.2   If the *client* decides to include such a statement:

(a)   advise and take instructions on whether the will is to be made conditional on the marriage or the formation of a *UK civil partnership* taking place; and

(b)   include appropriate statements in the will.

11.4   Executors and trustees

11.4.1   Explain to the *client*:

      (a)   the role and responsibilities of executors and trustees;

      (b)   the skills required;

      (c)   the reasons why it may be appropriate to appoint more than one executor and/or a substitute; and

      (d)   the importance of selecting individuals who can work together harmoniously.

11.4.2   Inform the *client* that executors and trustees can be either professionals (who will charge for their services) or lay persons such as family members or beneficiaries.

11.4.3   Explain that lay persons appointed as executors and/or trustees have the option of engaging a professional to assist them in the *administration of the estate*.

11.4.4   Before suggesting that the *client* can appoint the *will drafter* or members of the *will drafter's practice* as executors and/or trustees, take into account the *client's* best interests. For example, if the estate is small or straightforward, it may not be in the *client's* best interests to appoint a professional as the executor.

11.4.5   If the *client* is considering appointing members of the *will drafter's practice*, explain what the current cost would be if the *will drafter's practice* carried out the *administration of the estate*:

      (a)   on behalf of a lay executor; or

      (b)   as an appointed executor and/or trustee.

11.4.6   Make it clear to the *client*:

      (a)   whether the fees quoted are based on an hourly rate and/or a percentage of the estate;

      (b)   whether the amount quoted is for the work involved in administering the estate or is simply the fee for acting as an executor and supervising others doing the necessary work; and

      (c)   that these fees may change in the future.

11.4.7   Where there may be a continuing role as a trustee, make clear to the *client* any trustee fees that may be relevant to the estate.

11.4.8   Inform the *client* that appointment of the *will drafter* or the *will drafter's practice* as an executor and/or trustee is not compulsory.

11.4.9   Where a *client* decides to appoint members of the *will drafter's practice* as executors and/or trustees, record the *client's* reasons for the appointment and preserve as part of the will file. This will assist the *practice* in making a decision if asked in the future to renounce probate.

11.4.10   Where a will appoints a member of the *will drafter's practice* as a named executor, record the appointment centrally so that steps can be taken if the person named dies or leaves the *practice*.

11.4.11   Where a will appoints a partner or employee of the *will drafter's practice* as executor and/or trustee and the will includes a clause exonerating the executor and/or trustee from liability for negligence:

    (a)   fully explain the effect of the clause to the *client*;

    (b)   provide the *client* with a written record of the explanation; and

    (c)   preserve a copy of the record as part of the will file.

11.4.12   Where a *client* directs that an executor is to receive a legacy, establish whether the legacy is conditional on acting as executor and include a statement in the will to make the position clear.

11.4.13   Draft appropriate clauses to give effect to the *client's* wishes.

Note:

(i)   See the Law Society's Appointment of a Professional Executor Practice Note.

11.5   Guardians

11.5.1   Ascertain whether:

    (a)   the *client* has *parental responsibility* for a *minor*;

    (b)   the *client* has been appointed as a *guardian* of a *minor*; and

    (c)   the *client* has already made an appointment of a *guardian*.

11.5.2   Give advice to the *client* on:

    (a)   what happens if no appointment is made;

    (b)   that an appointment can be made by will or by separate written document which is signed and dated;

    (c)   when an appointment takes effect; and

    (d)   the rights of the *minor's* other parent.

11.5.3   If the *client* is uncertain of who to select as a *guardian*:

    (a)   discuss the advantages and disadvantages of the various possibilities to assist the *client* in making a choice; and

    (b)   advise the *client* to check that the person(s) chosen are willing to act.

11.5.4   Help the *client* to decide:

(**a**)   whether any funds available to meet the needs of the *minors* should be settled for the benefit of the *minors* or left to them absolutely or contingently;

(**b**)   where funds are settled, whether it is appropriate to appoint the *guardians* or separate individuals as trustees of any funds to be held for the *minors*; and

(**c**)   if separate trustees are to be appointed, what powers they will have to make funds available to the *guardians*.

11.5.5   Discuss with the *client* the preparation of a letter of wishes for the trustees and/or *guardians* and, if the preparation of this letter is outside the *practice's* standard *will drafting* retainer, ensure that the charge for this additional work is made clear to the *client* before any action is taken.

11.5.6   Draft appropriate clauses for the will, or separate appointment of *guardians* and, if requested, the letter of wishes.

11.6   Personal chattels

11.6.1   Where settling the whole estate or a substantial part of it on trust, make a separate gift of personal chattels unless there is a particular reason for including them within the settlement.

11.6.2   Inform the *client* that the ownership of personal chattels can give rise to arguments after death and give advice on the need to clarify ownership and resolve any uncertainty, particularly in relation to lent or borrowed items.

11.6.3   Establish whether any chattels are used partly for personal and partly for business purposes and, if so, how the *client* wants to deal with such assets, and draft appropriately.

11.6.4   Where individuals are being given a power of selection, include:

(**a**)   a time period within which the selection must be made; and

(**b**)   power for personal representatives to resolve any disputes.

11.6.5   If a *client* is preparing an informal letter of wishes to deal with personal chattels, advise the *client* of the need:

(**a**)   for accurate identification of items;

(**b**)   to keep the letter up-to-date; and

(**c**)   to ensure that the letter can be found after death.

11.7   Substitutional gifts and survivorship clauses

11.7.1   Encourage *clients* to consider what they want to happen if beneficiaries die before or shortly after the *client*.

11.7.2   Draft appropriately, bearing in mind that, in the case of spouses and civil partners, a survivorship clause may result in the payment of unnecessary inheritance tax:

(a)   where one estate is above and one below the inheritance tax threshold; and

(b)   where the couple die in circumstances where it is uncertain who died first.

11.8   Gifts to minors

11.8.1   In the case of gifts to *minors*, establish the following and draft appropriately:

(a)   Whether the executor is to accept the receipt of a parent or *guardian* or the *minor* at a specified age.

(b)   Where funds are to be held on trust by specified trustees or by the executors, the extent to which capital and income can be made available to the beneficiary.

(c)   Where gifts are to be made to a class, for example 'to my grandchildren', whether any provision is to be made for those born after the *client's* death and whether the *client* wants 'step' relatives to be included.

(d)   Where gifts are to be made to the children of different parents, whether:

(i)   each child is to receive the same amount irrespective of the number of siblings (a 'per capita' distribution); or

(ii)   an amount is to be divided amongst each set of siblings (a 'per stirpes' distribution); or

(iii)   the distribution is to be on any other basis, such as under Sharia law.

11.9   Gifts of specific assets

11.9.1   Explain the effect of ademption.

11.9.2   Establish whether the *client* wants:

(a)   the beneficiary to take only a particular asset;

(b)   the beneficiary to take any asset fulfilling a general description; and

(c) to include a substitutional gift to take effect if the original gift is adeemed.

11.9.3 If the *client* wishes to make a specific gift of an asset (such as the house in which they are living), advise the *client* of the risk that they may sell the asset and die without making a new will to deal with the changed circumstances.

11.9.4 In the case of gifts of shares in private companies:

(a) ask the *client* whether there are any pre-emption rights and, if so, discuss whether the gift is satisfactory in light of those rights;

(b) if the *client* wishes to include the gift despite the existence of such rights, or while uncertain as to the position:

    (i) record the discussion in writing;

    (ii) provide the *client* with a copy; and

    (iii) preserve the record as part of the will file.

11.9.5 Establish whether any assets which are to be specifically given are subject to any mortgage or charge and, if so, whether the *client* wants:

(a) the liability to be discharged from the residue of the estate; or

(b) the liability to fall on the specific beneficiary;

and draft appropriately.

11.10 Pecuniary legacies

11.10.1 Advise the *client* that gifts of specified amounts carry risks if the will is not kept under review, including:

(a) that inflation may mean the amount given is inadequate for its intended purpose at the date of death; and

(b) the erosion of capital may mean that the amount given represents a disproportionately high proportion of the estate by the date of death.

11.10.2 Discuss with the *client* whether a gift of a proportion of the estate would be more satisfactory.

11.10.3 Where a *client* wants to make a gift of an amount equal to his/her available nil-rate band at the date of death:

(a) establish whether they may have transferred nil-rate band available at the date of death;

(b) establish whether the legacy is to include the benefit of any such transferred nil-rate band; and

(c) draft appropriately.

11.10.4 Unless the amount of the legacy is very small, make express provision for the payment of interest, if any, on pecuniary legacies rather than relying on implied rules.

11.10.5 Consider with the *client* whether legacies should be absolute, contingent or settled and draft appropriately.

11.11 Burden of inheritance tax on non-residuary gifts

11.11.1 Where inheritance tax is likely to be payable on an estate:

(a) explain that, unless the will provides otherwise, the inheritance tax attributable to non-residuary gifts is payable from the residue of the estate;

(b) establish whether this is what the *client* wants; and

(c) draft accordingly.

11.12 Gifts to charity

11.12.1 Where a *client* gives an instruction for a gift to a charity:

(a) establish its correct name, address and registration number and whether it is incorporated or unincorporated;

(b) establish what the *client* wants to happen to the legacy if the charity has amalgamated, ceased to exist or become subject to a winding-up order before death, and draft appropriately;

(c) if inheritance tax is likely to be payable on the part of the estate not passing to charity, explain in outline:

(i) the effect of the reduced rate of inheritance tax;

(ii) the requirements for obtaining it; and

(iii) the possibility of drafting the charitable gift by reference to a formula clause to maximise the chance that the relief will be available on death.

11.12.2 Provide any further advice necessary and draft the legacy to give effect to the *client's* wishes.

11.12.3 Where the *client* instructs that the residue is to be divided 'equally' between charitable and non-charitable legatees, ensure that the drafting makes it clear whether the 'equal' division is before or after taking into account any inheritance tax to be borne by the non-charitable legatees.

Note:

(i)   See *Charities as Beneficiaries* 3rd edition (Law Society, 2012).

11.13   Powers of appointment

11.13.1   Establish whether the *client* has any powers of appointment exercisable by will and, if so, the terms of such powers.

11.13.2   Even if the *client* wishes the property to pass to the person entitled in default of appointment, make an express appointment so that there is no uncertainty as to the *client's* intention.

11.14   Option to purchase

11.14.1   Take particular care with options to purchase as they require the *client* to make a number of decisions and careful drafting to reflect those decisions.

11.14.2   Establish the following and ensure that the clause drafted is appropriate to meet the *client's* wishes:

(a)   A method for determining the price.
(b)   Whether the valuation is to be market value or a discounted value.
(c)   Whether the value is to be determined at the date of death or whether subsequent events are to be taken into account.
(d)   If a named individual or firm is to carry out the valuation, what is to happen if the individual or firm is unable to do so.
(e)   How the grantee of the option is to be informed and whether any time limit imposed runs from the date of death or from the date of notification.
(f)   Whether any time limit is to be strictly complied with.

11.15   Gifts of residue

11.15.1   Help the *client* to assess whether the amount likely to pass under the terms of the residuary gift will be adequate once non-residuary gifts, inheritance tax and other liabilities have been considered.

11.15.2   Help the *client* to consider whether the residuary gift should be absolute or settled, taking into account factors such as:

(a)   the need to provide for the competing claims of children, spouses or cohabitees;
(b)   asset protection;
(c)   flexibility; and

(d)   the complexity and cost of managing a settlement.

11.15.3 If the *client* is considering the use of a settlement:

(a)   explain the relative merits of settlements with an interest in possession and accumulation and discretionary settlements;

(b)   explain the tax treatment of the different types of settlement; and

(c)   help the *client* make an appropriate choice.

11.15.4 Where residue is to be settled:

(a)   explain to the *client* that it is normally appropriate for the settlement to be made flexible by including wide powers for trustees to deal with income and capital; and

(b)   if instructed, include appropriate powers and explain their effect to the *client*.

11.15.5 Help the *client* to make an appropriate choice of trustee and to make the arrangements for appointing and removing trustees.

11.15.6 Where a beneficiary is to be a trustee, include express provisions setting out the circumstances in which a trustee with a beneficial interest can act.

11.15.7 Discuss with the *client* whether it is desirable to include a further gift of residue to take effect if the primary gift fails.

11.16   Administrative provisions

11.16.1 Include appropriate administrative provisions to facilitate the efficient *administration of the estate* and management of any trusts arising under the terms of the will.

11.16.2 Provide the *client* with an explanation in general terms of the effect of such provisions. Where the *practice* uses standard administrative provisions, it will be helpful to have prepared a standard explanation which can be included in the letter of explanation accompanying the will (or draft).

11.16.3 Provide a separate explanation of the reason for, and effect of, any non-standard provision included in the will.

12   PROBLEMS WITH THE AGREED TIME FRAME

12.1   If unexpected workloads, illness or unforeseen events mean that the person responsible for drafting the will cannot complete it within the agreed time frame, either:

(a) arrange for another member of the *practice* to do so, making sure that the instructions are clear and unambiguous and putting in place an arrangement for checking the work done; or

(b) renegotiate the time for delivery with the *client*, making sure that this does not carry any unacceptable risk for the *client*.

12.1.2 Ensure that the *client* is informed in writing of the name and status of the new person dealing with the matter as soon as possible.

13 CONFIRMING THE CLIENT'S INSTRUCTIONS

13.1 Before the will is executed, take the steps in obligations **13.2–13.4** below to establish that the will correctly carries out the *client's* instructions and that the *client* does not wish to amend those instructions.

13.2 Send the *client* either:

(a) a copy of the instructions for the will agreed at the interview; or

(b) a draft of the will together with a letter explaining its effect using clear, understandable language and avoiding technical terms and expressions.

13.3 In cases where the *client* has difficulty understanding written material, take appropriate steps to explain the draft. This will normally require a second visit unless alternative suitable arrangements have been agreed.

13.4 If the will is not written in the *client's* first language, ensure that the *client* understands the will. This may require an interpreter and consideration of whether the interpreter is sufficiently independent.

14 EXECUTION OF THE WILL

14.1 Offer the *client* a choice between:

(a) having the execution of the will supervised at the *will drafter's* office or by a home visit; or

(b) making his/her own arrangements for the execution of the will, with full written instructions provided by the *will drafter*.

14.2 Make clear whether the cost of supervised execution is included in the fee charged for preparation of the will.

14.3 If the *client* has a disability, consider whether the offer of a home visit is a reasonable adjustment (in which case a separate charge is unlawful under the Equality Act 2010, s.20(7)).

14.4   If the offer of supervised execution is declined, provide the *client* with clear and correct instructions on:

    (a)   choice of witnesses; and

    (b)   the procedure for signing and witnessing the will.

14.5   Offer to inspect the will (or a copy) without additional fee after unsupervised execution to check that:

    (a)   the formalities appear to have been correctly complied with; and

    (b)   the witnesses do not appear to be beneficiaries or spouses or civil partners of beneficiaries.

14.6   Carry out the inspection referred to in obligation **14.5** above as a matter of course where a will is returned to the *practice* for storage.

14.7   Where a will is to be signed on behalf of the testator/testatrix, take steps (either by supervising execution or by providing clear written instructions) to ensure that:

    (a)   the person signing does so in the presence of, and by the direction of, the testator/testatrix; and

    (b)   the testator/testatrix indicates that he/she knows and approves the contents of the will;

and draft the attestation clause appropriately to recite that this happened.

14.8   Before going to the *client's* house or to a hospital or care home to supervise execution, enquire whether suitable individuals will be available to act as witnesses and, if not, make appropriate arrangements to have suitable witnesses available.

14.9   Where the *client* had sufficient testamentary capacity to give instructions for a will but has deteriorated by the time the will is to be executed and may not recover, assess whether the will can be executed under the rule in *Parker* v. *Felgate*, despite the lack of full testamentary capacity. This rule requires establishing whether the *client*:

    (a)   remembers giving instructions for the will; and

    (b)   understands that the will has been prepared in accordance with those instructions.

Note:

(i)   See *Parker* v. *Felgate* (1883) LR 8 PD 171.

15   CLIENTS WHO DO NOT PROCEED WITH EXECUTION OF THE WILL

15.1   If a *client* does not respond within a reasonable period after the *practice* has sent a draft will for approval or a will for execution, write to the *client*:

    (a)   explaining that the *will drafter* has carried out the terms of the retainer and will take no further steps unless instructed to do so;

    (b)   explaining that the *will drafter* will make any alterations to the will that the *client* gives instructions for; and

    (c)   reminding the *client* of the way in which the estate will devolve if the will is not executed.

15.2   Send two further reminder letters, at reasonable intervals, and if nothing further is heard from the *client*, present a bill for the work done.

16   STORAGE OF NEW AND PREVIOUS WILLS

16.1   Explain to the *client* the importance of informing those who will deal with the *administration of the estate* of the location of the will. Recommend the use of the Law Society's Personal Assets Log, or similar document, to convey this information, and consider with the *client* the option to use a wills registration service.

16.2   Inform the *client* that wills can be stored with:

    (a)   the *will drafter's practice*, if offering this service;

    (b)   the Probate Registry under the Senior Courts Act 1981, s.126;

    (c)   a bank;

    (d)   the *client*;

    (e)   a commercial provider.

16.3   Discuss with the *client* what is to happen to previous wills to ensure that there is a record of previous testamentary dispositions while limiting the risk of a revoked will being proved by mistake.

16.4   If the *will drafter's practice* operates a storage facility:

    (a)   ensure that the *client* understands that use of the service is not compulsory;

    (b)   make clear the basis of any charges;

    (c)   ensure that any charges are fair and reasonable;

    (d)   provide the *client* with a copy of the will and a note to be kept with the copy explaining where the original is stored;

    (e)   inform *clients* if the *practice* changes its name or ceases trading or ceases to offer a will storage facility;

      (f)   ensure that there is an efficient registration system so that wills can be retrieved when required;

      (g)   ensure that wills are stored securely in appropriate conditions; and

      (h)   limit persons who can access wills.

17   CLOSING THE FILE

17.1   Return any documents to which the *client* is entitled.

17.2   Review the file to ensure that documents and correspondence are filed correctly and discard any scrap or duplicate copies.

17.3   If storing the original will, ensure that it is registered in accordance with the registration system operated by the *practice*.

17.4   Store the contents of the file in accordance with the *practice's* file retention policy.

17.5   Retain the file until all risk of a claim has passed.

Note:

(i)   See the Law Society's File Retention: Wills and Probate Practice Note.

18   LATER DISPUTES

18.1   Where there is a serious dispute as to the validity of a will, make the attendance note (and any other relevant information) available to anyone who has an interest in challenging the will in accordance with the decision in *Larke* v. *Nugus*.

Notes:

(i)   See *Larke* v. *Nugus* (2000) WTLR 1033.
(ii)   See the Law Society's Disputed Wills Practice Note.

PART B

GENERAL ESTATE ADMINISTRATION

19   BEFORE ACCEPTING INSTRUCTIONS

19.1   Possible insolvency

19.1.1   Consider whether it is appropriate to carry out a 'bankruptcy only' search against the deceased at the Land Registry's Land Charges Department online or by using Form K16. Ensure that the search is made in the correct name of the deceased and try to ascertain whether the deceased used more than one version of his/her name. If so, search against all versions.

19.1.2   If there is a probability that the estate will be insolvent, consider whether it is in the *client's* best interests to let a creditor take the grant.

19.2   All assets passing by survivorship

19.2.1   If all assets are passing by survivorship, professional advice may not be required. However, if there is inheritance tax to pay, consider whether it may be in the *client's* best interests to have professional advice.

19.3   Complexity of the estate

19.3.1   Assess whether there are aspects of the estate which may be beyond your *practice's* expertise, for example:

    (a)   litigation arising from lifetime disputes;

    (b)   disputes as to the validity of the will;

    (c)   disputes as to the ownership of assets apparently included in the estate;

    (d)   a foreign element, such as a deceased domiciled outside England and Wales, or non-resident in UK or owning foreign assets; and

    (e)   assets requiring 'specialist' knowledge such as copyright, patents, royalties and mineral rights.

19.3.2   If so, suggest that the *client* takes separate advice and, if the *practice* has relevant knowledge, assist the *client* to identify a suitable adviser, but consider whether it is in the *client's* best interests for the *practice* to cease to act in relation to the *estate administration*.

19.4   Initial assessment of validity of any will

19.4.1   Where there is a will, establish whether there is any apparent reason to doubt its validity. In particular, examine the attestation clause, if any, and the signatures of the testator/testatrix and witnesses to establish whether the will appears to have been validly executed.

19.5   Money laundering suspicions

19.5.1   Assess whether there are any grounds for suspecting that assets of the estate may derive from criminal activity and, if so, whether those suspicions should be disclosed to the *practice's* nominated officer before deciding whether to accept instructions.

19.6   Contracts made 'off premises'

19.6.1   Where a contract for *estate administration* services is not made at the *practice's* office, comply with the Cancellation of Contracts made in a Consumer's Home or Place of Work etc. Regulations 2008 (as summarised in obligation **1.7** above).

Note:

(i)   See the Law Society's Cancellation of Contracts Practice Note.

20   MEMBERS OF THE PRACTICE APPOINTED AS EXECUTORS

20.1   Requests for renunciation

20.1.1   Where members of the *practice* have been appointed as executors and/or trustees, and are requested by beneficiaries of the estate to renounce probate, consider such requests in light of the *practice's* renunciation policy (see **EP.2** in **Part H** below).

20.1.2   No steps which could amount to intermeddling and, therefore, acceptance of the office of executor are to be taken while such requests are being considered.

20.2   Charges

20.2.1   Ensure that the charges made for acting as executor (and, if relevant, trustee) are fair and reasonable having regard to all the circumstances of the matter.

20.2.2   Where there are no lay co-executors, clearly explain in writing to all those with an entitlement to share in the residuary estate:

(a)   the basis of charging; and
(b)   all likely disbursements;

making it clear whether charges are calculated only on a time basis and/or include a value element.

20.3   Time frame

20.3.1   As soon as practicable after ascertaining beneficiaries:

(a)   inform them of their interest and, if established, its approximate extent;
(b)   give an estimate of the time frame for the *administration of the estate* and any time constraints that will affect it; and
(c)   give an explanation of the frequency of communication.

21   TAKING INSTRUCTIONS FROM PERSONAL REPRESENTATIVES

21.1   Charges

21.1.1   Charge on a fair and reasonable basis having regard to all the circumstances of the matter.

21.1.2   Clearly explain in writing to those giving instructions to act:

(a)   the basis of charging; and
(b)   all likely disbursements;

making it clear whether charges are calculated only on a time basis and/or include a value element.

21.1.3   Clearly explain in writing to those giving instructions to act whether the retainer is for obtaining the grant and dealing with the entire *administration of the estate* or whether it is limited to particular aspects of the process and, if limited, exactly what elements are included and excluded.

21.2 Entitlement to act

21.2.1 Consider with those giving instructions to act whether it is necessary to employ genealogists to trace family members and, if so, what charging structure is appropriate.

21.2.2 If the will appears to be valid, ascertain whether those with the best right to a grant are willing to act and, if not, who is going to take a grant.

21.2.3 In the case of a full or partial intestacy, once the family members are identified, ascertain whether those with the best right to a grant are willing to act and, if not, who is going to take a grant.

21.2.4 Advise whether more than one administrator is required.

21.2.5 If instructed to act for a person who does not have the best right to take a grant, take any steps necessary to clear off persons with a prior right. This may involve:

(a) obtaining a renunciation from those with a prior right; or
(b) issuing a citation; or
(c) making an application to pass over the person with the prior right.

21.2.6 If the person with the best right to a grant feels unable to act as a personal representative, discuss whether it is in his/her best interests to:

(a) renounce; or
(b) appoint an attorney.

21.3 Uncertainty as to whether the deceased made a will

21.3.1 Advise the *client* on the steps that can be taken to search for a will. These will normally include:

(a) searching the house;
(b) contacting the deceased's banks, former professional advisers and local law society;
(c) advertising;
(d) commissioning a commercial provider to undertake a search; and
(e) checking whether the deceased deposited the will with the Probate Registry.

21.4   Supporting affidavits

21.4.1   Determine whether any affidavits are required (e.g. an affidavit as to due execution where there is no attestation clause or the attestation clause is defective) and, if so, prepare any necessary affidavit.

21.4.2   Give clear instructions to the person(s) making the affidavit as to the steps necessary to swear or affirm and, if necessary, make arrangements for them to swear or affirm.

21.5   Renunciations

21.5.1   Where those with prior rights to take a grant wish to renounce, either:

(**a**)   prepare the renunciation; or

(**b**)   make arrangements for obtaining the renunciation if prepared by someone else.

21.6   Power reserved

21.6.1   Where some of those appointed as executors wish to have power reserved to take the grant at a later stage, serve notice of the application for a grant.

21.7   Powers of attorney

21.7.1   Where the person with the best right to take a grant wishes to authorise someone to take a grant under a power of attorney, either:

(**a**)   draft the power of attorney, give clear instructions as to execution and check that it has been properly executed; or

(**b**)   if someone else prepared the power of attorney, check that it is correctly worded and has been correctly executed.

21.7.2   Be aware of the potential for financial abuse where an elderly person wishes to appoint an attorney for the purposes of taking out a grant of probate or letters of administration.

Note:

(i)   See the Law Society's Financial Abuse Practice Note.

21.8   Duties and responsibilities of personal representatives

21.8.1   Advise those proposing to act as personal representatives:

(a) that criminal and civil sanctions will arise:

  (i)   if a will or codicil is concealed; and
  (ii) if false information is provided about the assets of the estate, lifetime gifts, those who may be entitled to share in the estate or those entitled;

(b) of the steps involved in obtaining a grant and dealing with the *administration of an estate*;

(c) of their duty to ascertain and secure the assets and liabilities of the estate;

(d) of their duty to distribute the estate correctly;

(e) of their duty to calculate and arrange for the payment of the inheritance tax due;

(f) of the risk that penalties will be imposed on them if they provide inaccurate information to HM Revenue and Customs;

(g) of their potential liability to creditors and beneficiaries of the estate in the event of maladministration; and

(h) whether a continuing trust will arise.

21.9 Customer due diligence

21.9.1 Carry out appropriate customer due diligence on personal representatives.

22 DISPUTED VALIDITY OF A WILL

22.1 In the event of a dispute as to the validity of a will, determine what steps are appropriate and advise accordingly.

22.2 Consider whether the *practice* has the necessary expertise to deal with a contentious probate matter. If not, suggest the *client* obtains separate advice and, if the *practice* has relevant knowledge, assist the *client* to find a suitable adviser.

22.3 If someone in the *practice* drafted the disputed will and there is an allegation of negligence, inform all interested parties without delay of the need to obtain independent advice and cease to act in relation to the dispute.

22.4 If there is a serious dispute as to the validity of a will prepared by the *practice*, make all information relating to the circumstances in which the will was made and executed available to those with an interest in the dispute.

22.5 Inform the *practice's* professional indemnity insurer.

Note:

(i)   See the Law Society's Disputed Wills Practice Note.

23   IMMEDIATE ACTION TO PROTECT THE ESTATE

23.1   Identify all necessary immediate action and either arrange it or advise personal representatives to arrange it. Such action will normally include the following steps, set out in obligations **23.2–23.13** below, as appropriate.

23.2   Register the death.

23.3   Check in the deceased's will (if any) or elsewhere for any expressions of wishes as to the funeral.

23.4   Make funeral arrangements and explore the possibility of paying funeral expenses directly from the deceased's bank or building society accounts.

23.5   Secure the deceased's real property and possessions by:

    (a)   arranging buildings and contents insurance;
    (b)   changing locks, if appropriate;
    (c)   redirecting post;
    (d)   securing the fabric of buildings by adjusting the heating and draining the water system as appropriate;
    (e)   arranging a house-sitter for the property before the time of the obituary/funeral, if appropriate;
    (f)   taking photographs of home contents;
    (g)   removing particularly valuable items and arranging for secure storage;
    (h)   making appropriate arrangements for certified firearms;
    (i)   cancelling regular deliveries;
    (j)   notifying the landlord and local authority, as appropriate; and
    (k)   notifying tenants and/or management company.

23.6   Arrange care for livestock and pets.

23.7   Determine whether any assets can be realised without a grant of representation and, if so, take steps to obtain payment.

23.8   Open a bank account to be operated by the personal representatives unless all cash is to be paid into the *practice's* client account.

23.9   Discuss what is to happen to personal chattels and, where the deceased lived alone, house contents.

23.10   Make arrangements for the disposal of perishable items and rubbish.

23.11   Inform the Office of the Public Guardian and the Court of Protection if there was a lasting power of attorney or enduring power of attorney or deputyship order.

23.12   Ascertain what steps need to be taken to identify and realise digital assets.

23.13   Establish whether any UK beneficiary is bankrupt. When carrying out any bankruptcy searches, ensure that the search is made in the correct name of the beneficiary and try to ascertain whether the beneficiary uses more than one version of his/her name. If so, search against all versions. Consider whether it is necessary to take advice on the need for searches against non-UK beneficiaries.

Note:

(i)   See the Law Society's Bankrupt Beneficiaries Practice Note.

24   ADVICE ON STATE BENEFITS

24.1   Where appropriate, provide advice to family and/or personal representatives on claiming:

(a)   funeral payment;
(b)   bereavement payment; and
(c)   bereavement or widowed parent's allowance.

25   PREPARING TO APPLY FOR A GRANT OF REPRESENTATION

25.1   Collecting information

25.1.1   Contact stockbrokers, accountants and other professional advisers instructed by the deceased as to the assets of the estate.

25.1.2   Warn those acting as personal representatives that if they give inaccurate information to HM Revenue and Customs, which results in an underpayment of inheritance tax, they are likely to have to pay penalties.

25.1.3   Take steps to ensure that:

(a)   family members; and
(b)   others of whom enquiries are made;

are aware that, if they give inaccurate information to personal representatives which results in an underpayment of inheritance tax, they are likely to have to pay penalties.

25.1.4   Obtain all possible information from family members and professional advisers on assets owned at the date of the death, including those owned as beneficial joint tenants.

25.1.5   Where an estate is, or may be, chargeable to inheritance tax, ascertain whether the deceased inherited any assets in the five years before death to establish the availability of quick succession relief.

25.1.6   Write to asset holders to establish exact values at the date of death.

25.1.7   Instruct qualified valuers to provide open market valuations of assets such as land and specialist chattels.

25.1.8   Obtain information on the liabilities of the deceased at the date of death.

25.1.9   Write to known creditors to establish the exact amount owing at the date of death.

25.1.10   Ascertain the cost of the funeral and other testamentary expenses.

25.1.11   Obtain information on lifetime transfers made by the deceased within seven years before death.

25.1.12   If any transfer made within seven years of death was immediately chargeable, obtain information on any transfers made by the deceased within seven years before that transfer.

25.1.13   Where the deceased was a surviving spouse or civil partner, establish whether there is any unused nil-rate band available from the estate of the first to die.

25.1.14   Obtain information on any assets which may qualify for business or agricultural relief or any other relief, such as that available on growing timber.

25.1.15   Establish whether any assets qualify for heritage property relief and whether those entitled to such assets are willing to give the necessary undertakings.

25.1.16   Establish whether any assets are passing to exempt beneficiaries, such as spouses, civil partners, charities or political parties.

25.1.17 Be alert to the possibility that estate assets may be the proceeds of crime (e.g. welfare benefits to which the deceased was not entitled) and, if you acquire knowledge or become suspicious:

    (a) make immediate disclosure to the *practice's* nominated officer; and

    (b) continue to act but do not transfer funds or take any other irrevocable step.

Note:

(i) See the Law Society's Anti-Money Laundering Practice Note.

25.2   Foreign assets

25.2.1 If there is a foreign will, check its terms for inconsistency with the last will and codicils made by the deceased in England and Wales.

25.2.2 Advise lay personal representatives or, if none, residuary beneficiaries, that specialist assistance may be necessary to realise foreign assets and that the foreign jurisdictions may not recognise the status of personal representatives.

25.2.3 Advise those apparently entitled under the terms of a will or under the intestacy rules that there may be forced heirship rights and, if appropriate, suggest that the *client* obtains legal advice in the relevant jurisdiction.

25.2.4 Once entitlement to foreign assets is established, consider if the *practice* has the necessary expertise to obtain the assets and, if so, take instructions.

25.2.5 If the *practice* does not have the necessary expertise, suggest that the *client* obtains separate advice and, if the *practice* has relevant knowledge, assist the *client* to identify a suitable adviser, but consider whether in the best interests of the *client* the *practice* should cease acting in relation to the *administration of the estate*.

25.3   Insolvent estate

25.3.1 If the estate appears to be insolvent, explain the implications to those proposing to act as personal representatives and advise that it may be preferable to allow a creditor to take the grant.

26 APPLYING FOR A GRANT OF REPRESENTATION

26.1 Inheritance tax account and calculation of the inheritance tax due

26.1.1 Carry out the steps in obligations **26.1.2–26.1.7** below to complete the inheritance tax account and calculate the inheritance tax due as appropriate.

26.1.2 If the inheritance tax is due, apply for an inheritance tax reference number at least three weeks before the expected date for payment either online or by submitting Form IHT 422 by post.

26.1.3 If the estate qualifies as an excepted estate, complete Form IHT 205.

26.1.4 If the estate is not excepted, complete Form IHT 400 or Form IHT 401 and all necessary supporting schedules.

26.1.5 Calculate any inheritance tax due.

26.1.6 Arrange for personal representatives to sign and date the relevant account.

26.1.7 Liaise with trustees of any trust in which the deceased had an interest in possession.

26.2 Arrangements for payment of the inheritance tax due

26.2.1 Consider whether the instalment option is available on any assets of the estate and, if so, whether it is appropriate to claim it.

26.2.2 Pay the inheritance tax due as quickly as possible to prevent unnecessary payment of interest.

26.2.3 If there is a delay in calculating the exact amount due, consider with the personal representatives and interested beneficiaries whether it is appropriate to make a payment on account.

26.2.4 Consider with the personal representatives and interested beneficiaries whether it is possible to tender assets in satisfaction of the inheritance tax liability under the Inheritance Tax Act 1984, s.230 and, if so, whether this is desirable.

26.2.5 Make arrangements for paying any inheritance tax due as cost effectively as possible. This may be by arranging:

(a) to obtain the grant on credit;

(b) direct payment from a bank, building society or National Savings and Investments;

(c) payment of assets realisable without a grant of representation;

(d) borrowing from a beneficiary; or

(e) borrowing from a bank or building society.

26.2.6 Diarise dates for payment of future instalments of inheritance tax.

26.3   The Oath

26.3.1 Complete an appropriate Oath containing all necessary information.

26.3.2 Where there are lay personal representatives, give clear instructions as to the steps necessary to swear or affirm the Oath and, if necessary, make arrangements for them to swear or affirm.

26.4   Submission of the inheritance tax account

26.4.1 Submit the following to HM Revenue and Customs:

(a) Form IHT 400 or IHT 401 and accompanying schedules.

(b) Any inheritance tax due, either by cheque or by electronic transfer using the inheritance tax reference number previously obtained.

26.5   Obtaining the grant

26.5.1 Consider whether there are circumstances which make it appropriate to search the index of caveats before applying for a grant.

26.5.2 Submit to the Probate Registry:

(a) the Oath;

(b) the last will or wills together with any codicils, signed by the personal representatives as exhibits to the Oath;

(c) two unbound A4 copies of each testamentary document;

(d) any affidavits, renunciations of the right to take a grant and powers of attorney required;

(e) the receipted Form IHT 421 or Form IHT 205; and

(f) the probate fee.

26.5.3 Where an application cannot proceed because a caveat has been lodged, consider whether the *practice* has the necessary expertise to deal with a probate dispute. If not, suggest that the *client* obtains separate advice and, if the *practice* has relevant knowledge, assist the *client* to identify a suitable adviser.

26.5.4   Order sufficient official copies of the grant of representation to enable swift and efficient *administration of the estate*.

27   ADVISING ON BENEFICIAL ENTITLEMENT

27.1   Advising personal representatives where there is a will

27.1.1   Advise personal representatives on the correct construction of the will and its effect. Typically this will include advice on the following matters:

    (a)   whether gifts have failed, which may have happened for a number of reasons, including:

        (i)   a beneficiary, spouse or civil partner of a beneficiary witnessed the will;

        (ii)   divorce or dissolution of a *UK civil partnership*;

        (iii)   ademption;

        (iv)   lapse;

        (v)   failure to survive a required period;

        (vi)   uncertainty;

        (vii)   contrary to public policy; or

        (viii)   forfeiture;

    (b)   whether gifts are absolute or contingent;

    (c)   whether gifts carry the right to intermediate income or interest;

    (d)   the extent of property passing under the terms of particular gifts;

    (e)   the identity of beneficiaries;

    (f)   the identity of members of a class of beneficiaries;

    (g)   whether the will creates a trust and, if so, the terms of the trust;

    (h)   whether the will was made in pursuance of a mutual wills agreement as a result of which the other party to the agreement is now bound by its terms;

    (i)   whether the will contains a half-secret trust;

    (j)   the extent to which inheritance tax is to be paid from residue or is borne by the non-residuary beneficiary;

    (k)   any ambiguities which may require counsel's opinion and/or the direction of the court; and

    (l)   the destination of any property passing independently of the will, such as:

        (i)   property passing by survivorship or under the terms of a lifetime trust;

        (ii)   the proceeds of life assurance policies written in trust or assigned during the lifetime of the deceased;

        (iii)   lump sums payable from pension schemes;

    (iv)   death in service benefits; and

    (v)   property passing under the intestacy rules where there is a partial intestacy.

27.1.2   Agree any steps that need to be taken, such as obtaining counsel's opinion, and take appropriate action.

27.2   Advising personal representatives where property passes under the intestacy rules

27.2.1   Explain to personal representatives:

    (a)   who is entitled to share the estate;

    (b)   the extent of their entitlement; and

    (c)   whether their interests are vested or contingent.

27.2.2   If relevant, explain to a surviving spouse or civil partner:

    (a)   the effect of a life interest;

    (b)   his/her right to capitalise a life interest, dealing with the points set out at obligation **38.1** below;

    (c)   his/her right to take any dwelling house passing on intestacy in which he/she was resident at the date of death in or toward satisfaction of his/her interest in the estate;

    (d)   his/her right to make an application under the Inheritance (Provision for Family and Dependants) Act 1975.

27.3   Communication with beneficiaries and creditors

27.3.1   On obtaining the grant, review the assets and liabilities. If payment of liabilities cannot be made within 28 days of obtaining the grant, write to the creditors of the position.

27.3.2   Within 10 working days of obtaining the grant, or within such other time frame set by the *practice* which ensures consistently prompt action in this regard, communicate with beneficiaries to:

    (a)   remind them of their interest and, if established, its approximate extent;

    (b)   give an estimate of the time frame for distribution and any time constraints that will affect it;

    (c)   give an explanation of the frequency of communication;

    (d)   if appropriate, ask for instructions as to whether they want assets encashed or transferred in specie.

28   PROTECTION AGAINST CREDITORS AND CLAIMANTS

28.1   Consider what steps, if any, are appropriate to ascertain creditors and claimants and protect personal representatives from liability. Possible steps include:

(a)   statutory advertisements; or

(b)   insurance.

28.2   If statutory advertisements have been placed, record the date of the advertisement, the time frame for claims and preserve copies of the paperwork in the file.

29   COLLECTING THE ASSETS

29.1   Unless instructed otherwise, without delay, write to holders of cash such as banks, building societies and National Savings and Investments enclosing an official copy of the grant (unless the institution will accept a certified copy) and asking for payment of the amount due.

29.2   Ask for a separate note of any interest accrued since the date of death.

29.3   In the case of non-cash assets such as land and shares which are passing to beneficiaries, obtain and complete appropriate documentation to transfer title from the deceased to either the personal representatives or to the beneficiaries entitled.

29.4   In the case of foreign assets, ascertain (if necessary by instructing an expert in the relevant jurisdiction):

(a)   the steps required to realise the asset; and

(b)   the appropriate person to take them if the office of personal representative is not recognised.

Note:

(i)   See the Law Society's Estate Administration: Banking Protocols Practice Note.

30   PAYING THE DEBTS

30.1   With the authority of the personal representatives, as soon as cash is available, pay any outstanding debts of the estate and sums borrowed to meet the estate's liability for inheritance tax.

30.2   If there is any possibility that the estate may prove to be insolvent, follow the bankruptcy order when paying debts, as required by the Administration of Insolvent Estates of Deceased Persons Order 1986.

30.3   Unless a lay personal representative is taking the whole estate, establish whether there are any contingent or uncertain liabilities. If there are, in order to protect the personal representative, either:

> **(a)**   set aside sufficient assets to meet the liability, should the liability arise; or
>
> **(b)**   take indemnities from those who will receive assets from the estate to reimburse the personal representative should the liability arise and warn the personal representative of the limitations of indemnities; or
>
> **(c)**   arrange insurance cover; or
>
> **(d)**   apply to the court for directions.

30.4   Unless a lay personal representative is taking the whole estate, establish whether the deceased had a leasehold interest and, if so:

> **(a)**   pay all existing liabilities; and
>
> **(b)**   set aside a fund to meet any future claims that may be made in respect of any fixed and ascertained sum which the lessee agreed to lay out in the future.

Note:

(i)   See the Administration of Insolvent Estates of Deceased Persons Order 1986 (SI 1986/1999).

31   SELLING THE ASSETS

31.1   Discuss the issues in obligations **31.2–31.4** below with the personal representative and take instructions.

31.2   Sale for more than the value of the asset at the date of death

31.2.1   Consider whether the sale will be for more than the value of the asset at the date of death. If so, capital gains tax at the higher rate may be payable to the extent that the gain exceeds any available annual exemption of the personal representatives.

31.2.2   Consider whether tax can be saved by appropriating the asset to:

> **(a)**   a beneficiary that is a charity; or

(b) a beneficiary who has unused annual exemption or available losses; or

(c) a beneficiary who will pay tax at a lower rate than the personal representative.

31.2.3 If tax can be saved by appropriating the asset to a beneficiary:

(a) inform the relevant beneficiaries;

(b) appropriate or assent the asset to the agreed beneficiary; and

(c) make the sale on behalf of the beneficiary.

31.2.4 Ensure that there is a full written record of the appropriation and/or assent, and the instruction to sell.

31.3 Sale for less than the value of the asset at the date of death

31.3.1 If the estate has not made, and is not likely to make, any capital gains, consider whether it is preferable to appropriate the asset to a beneficiary and make the sale on behalf of that beneficiary.

31.3.2 If it is preferable to appropriate the asset to a beneficiary:

(a) inform the beneficiary;

(b) if agreement is reached, appropriate or assent the asset to the agreed beneficiary; and

(c) make the sale on behalf of the beneficiary.

31.3.3 Ensure that there is a full written record of the appropriation and/or assent, and the instruction to sell.

31.4 Sale of land or qualifying investments for less than value at date of death

31.4.1 Consider whether the value of 'qualifying investments' or an 'interest in land' (as defined in the Inheritance Tax Act 1984, ss.178 and 190) has fallen, with the result that the sale price will be less than the value at the date of death, making it possible to substitute the sale price for inheritance tax purposes.

31.4.2 If so, consider and advise on the extent to which any inheritance tax liability of the estate can be reduced by making a claim to substitute the sale price for the original inheritance tax value.

31.4.3 To obtain the maximum benefit from loss relief, plan:

(a) the timing of such sales;

(b) which assets should be sold by the personal representatives; and

(c) which assets should be transferred to beneficiaries.

31.4.4 Where appropriate, make a claim for loss relief using Form IHT 35 or Form IHT 38.

31.5 Selection of estate investments for sale

31.5.1 Consider whether it is necessary to select some of the estate investments for sale.

31.5.2 If it is necessary to select investments for sale, unless the *practice* is authorised to provide financial advice, advise the personal representative to consult an appropriately qualified adviser.

32 INCOME TAX

32.1 If instructed, and in accordance with your retainer, carry out the steps in obligations **32.2–32.4** below. Be aware that, although preparation of income tax liability may fall outside of your retainer, you must settle the income tax liability of the estate.

32.2 Income tax position of deceased

32.2.1 If necessary, make returns in respect of the income of the estate up to the date of death.

32.2.2 Establish whether the deceased owed income tax at the date of death or was entitled to a refund in relation to any income, including income from settled property in which the deceased had an interest.

32.2.3 Make a claim for a refund or pay the amount due.

32.2.4 Include the refund or liability on the inheritance tax account submitted or, if the account has already been submitted, consider whether it is necessary to submit a corrective account.

32.3 Income tax liability of estate

32.3.1 Record all income received together with any tax credit in the case of dividend, and tax deducted in the case of interest.

32.3.2   Record any interest paid for the 12 months following death on a loan to pay inheritance tax, in so far as it relates to the payment of tax on personalty vesting in the personal representatives.

32.3.3   Unless income tax is being dealt with by a third party, claim any refund due to the estate as a result of borrowing to pay inheritance tax.

32.3.4   Complete the estate and trust return if required. Where a return is not required, deal with the HM Revenue and Customs office that handled the deceased's tax affairs.

32.3.5   Pay any tax due.

32.4   Income entitlement of beneficiaries

Beneficiaries entitled to specific assets

32.4.1   Pay any income produced by the assets to the beneficiary entitled at the same time that the asset is transferred and also give the beneficiary any documentation received in relation to any income tax deducted.

Pecuniary legatees

32.4.2   Pay interest to legatees from 12 months after the date of the death, at the basic rate payable on funds held in court, unless:

  (a)   the legacy is contingent or deferred (in which case interest is payable only from the deferral date or the date when the contingency is fulfilled); or

  (b)   the will provides otherwise.

Residuary beneficiaries

32.4.3   Check the income tax position of residuary beneficiaries to see if they would prefer to receive income payments over more than one tax year and, if so, try to stagger income payments.

Income tax statements

32.4.4   Provide all beneficiaries receiving income from the estate with a statement of income tax paid.

33   DISTRIBUTING THE ASSETS AND PAYING PECUNIARY LEGACIES

33.1   Advise personal representatives on:

    (a)   their personal liability if they misdistribute the estate; and

    (b)   the protection they can obtain by waiting before distributing and by insuring against liabilities.

33.2   Advise personal representatives that they will be personally liable if they distribute assets without waiting for at least:

    (a)   two months from the placing of statutory advertisements in relation to creditors and unknown claimants to the estate; and

    (b)   six months from the date of the grant in the case of a family provision claim.

(Be aware that, as family provision claimants have four months from issue of the claim in which to serve it, waiting a further four months is required for absolute protection.)

33.3   Help personal representatives assess the level of risk that an early distribution entails and, if appropriate, explore the possibility of insurance.

33.4   In the case of beneficiaries who are known to have existed but who cannot be traced, or who refuse to accept payment but will not disclaim or vary their entitlement, be aware that advertisements are no protection. Therefore, to protect personal representatives against the risk of an untraced beneficiary appearing after distribution:

    (a)   take indemnities from those who will receive assets from the estate but also warn personal representatives of the limitations of indemnities; or

    (b)   arrange insurance cover; or

    (c)   apply to court for an order allowing distribution on the basis that the beneficiary has predeceased (a 'Benjamin order') or on a similar basis; or

    (d)   consider whether a beneficiary's refusal to accept payment amounts to a disclaimer by conduct; or

    (e)   check whether the Court Funds Office will accept payment.

33.5   Before transferring assets or paying cash to a beneficiary based in the UK, carry out 'bankruptcy only' searches at the Land Registry's Land Charges Department online or by using Form K16.

33.6   In the case of a beneficiary based in a foreign jurisdiction:

(a) consider whether it is advisable to seek appropriate professional advice on the need for searches equivalent to a UK bankruptcy search;

(b) carry out such searches before transferring assets or paying cash; and

(c) consult beneficiaries on payment arrangements to foreign jurisdictions and currency exchange issues.

33.7 Subject to the time constraints set out at obligation **33.2** above, transfer assets to non-residuary beneficiaries as soon as it becomes apparent that the assets are not required for the payment of liabilities.

33.8 In the case of residuary beneficiaries:

(a) consider whether interim estate accounts are appropriate;

(b) consider whether distributions can be made before preparation and approval of final estate accounts; and

(c) prepare interim estate accounts and make distributions as appropriate.

33.9 Beneficiaries who have been left specific assets may prefer to have the assets sold on their behalf, receiving the proceeds of sale instead. If beneficiaries make such a request, and the personal representatives are willing to comply with it, make the arrangements promptly and:

(a) record the instruction; and

(b) record the appropriation and/or assent of the asset to the beneficiary;

to ensure that it is clear the sale was on behalf of the beneficiary.

33.10 In the case of pecuniary legacies:

(a) check whether the beneficiaries would prefer to have an asset appropriated in, or towards, satisfaction of their entitlement;

(b) explain that the appropriation will be at market value at the date of the appropriation and give the beneficiary full information;

(c) obtain the beneficiary's consent to the appropriation unless the will removes this requirement; and

(d) where the beneficiary wants cash, obtain bank account details and make payment as soon as practicable.

33.11 When transferring assets to a beneficiary:

(a) send a confirmation of receipt for signature and return; and

(b) provide written details of the value of the assets at the date of death for use on later disposals in the calculation of capital gains tax.

34   PREPARING ESTATE ACCOUNTS

34.1   Keep accurate records throughout the period of the *administration of the estate* so you are aware of the financial position at any time and to enable the timely preparation of estate accounts.

34.2   The accounts should show:

(a)   the value of assets at the date of death;

(b)   profits and losses on the sale of assets during the administration period;

(c)   payments made during the administration period;

(d)   charges made by the *practice*;

(e)   transfers of assets made to non-residuary beneficiaries;

(f)   income receipts, including interest allowed on money held in the client account;

(g)   income payments;

(h)   interim distributions to residuary beneficiaries;

(i)   retention of funds to meet contingent or future liabilities; and

(j)   balance of capital and income due to residuary beneficiaries.

35   DISTRIBUTING THE RESIDUE OF THE ESTATE

35.1   Send the estate accounts to the personal representatives for approval together with the final bill.

35.2   Send residuary beneficiaries the estate accounts for approval.

35.3   Provide a copy of the bill to the residuary beneficiaries if members of the *practice* are the only personal representatives.

35.4   Once the residuary beneficiaries have approved the accounts, carry out the searches as required in obligations **33.5** and **33.6** above, and transfer the balance of assets and cash to them.

35.5   When transferring assets to the residuary beneficiaries, send a confirmation of receipt for signature and return.

35.6   Provide a Form R185 to the beneficiary with details of income distributed.

36 CLOSING THE FILE

36.1 Write a final letter to the personal representatives or, if members of the *practice* are the personal representatives, to the residuary beneficiaries explaining:

(**a**) what you have done;

(**b**) that you are closing your file;

(**c**) what tasks, if any, remain to be done (e.g. payment of inheritance tax instalments);

(**d**) what information and documents should be retained, for example:

(**i**) valuations of assets at the date of death for use on later disposals in the calculation of capital gains tax;

(**ii**) all documentation required for claiming the transferable nil-rate band.

36.2 Return any documents to which the personal representatives or residuary beneficiaries are entitled.

36.3 Review the file to ensure that documents and correspondence are filed and recorded correctly and discard any scrap or duplicate copies.

36.4 Store the contents of the file in accordance with the *practice's* file retention policy.

PART C

SPECIAL ASPECTS OF ADMINISTRATION

37 WHERE THE WILL CREATES A CONTINUING SETTLEMENT

37.1 Where the will creates a continuing settlement, *practices* appointed as, or instructed by, personal representatives must carry out the obligations set in **37.2–37.6** below. This will ensure that the assets settled are transferred into the legal ownership of trustees as quickly as possible, subject to the time constraints required for their protection.

37.2 Specific assets

37.2.1 Transfer assets to the trustees once it is apparent that the assets are not required to pay liabilities. Use the appropriate documentation for each asset.

37.2.2 Where personal representatives and trustees are the same people, mark the transition by using an assent or written appropriation.

37.3 Cash

37.3.1 Transfer cash to the trustees once it is apparent that it is not required to pay liabilities using a cheque or electronic transfer.

37.4 Debt or charge arrangements

37.4.1 Check whether the will authorises the executors to compel the trustees of a settlement to accept a debt or charge over residuary assets instead of cash.

37.4.2 Where this is the case, help the executors to decide, in light of any letter of wishes left by the deceased, whether it is in the best interests of the beneficiaries of the estate to exercise this right.

37.4.3   If the executors decide that it is beneficial, help them to decide whether to constitute the settlement with a debt or charge.

37.4.4   Draft the appropriate documentation to give effect to the debt or charge arrangement. This will normally consist of:

(**a**)   a record of the executors' decision;

(**b**)   a letter to the trustees of the settlement requiring them to accept the debt or charge and stating whether the debt will carry any interest or index-linking; and

(**c**)   a loan agreement confirming that the residuary beneficiary owes the stated amount to the trustees of the settlement, or a charge agreement confirming that the debt is charged on the residuary assets.

37.5   Residue

37.5.1   As soon as the residue is ascertained and the estate accounts are approved by the trustees of the residuary settlement, transfer assets to the trustees using the appropriate documentation for each asset.

37.5.2   Where personal representatives and trustees are the same people, it is still important to mark the transition. This should be done by using an assent or written appropriation.

37.6   Making appointments from settlements without an interest in possession within two years of death

37.6.1   In the case of settlements without an interest in possession, check whether the trustees have powers of appointment allowing funds to be appointed to beneficiaries absolutely, thereby bringing the settlement to an end.

37.6.2   If they do, consider with the trustees whether it is in the interests of the beneficiaries to terminate the settlement within two years of death and obtain 'reading back' for inheritance tax purposes.

37.6.3   Draft a memorandum setting out the trustees' decision and any deed of appointment required, taking care to wait three months from the date of death where necessary to obtain 'reading back' for inheritance tax purposes.

38 SETTLEMENTS ARISING UNDER THE INTESTACY RULES

38.1 Life interest for surviving spouse or civil partner

38.1.1 Where the intestacy rules produce a life interest for a spouse or civil partner, explain to the spouse or civil partner as soon as possible:

    (a) the effect of a life interest;

    (b) his/her right to capitalise the life interest within 12 months of the grant of representation; and

    (c) the procedure to be followed to exercise the right.

38.1.2 Once the size of the life interest fund is known, calculate the capital sum that would be payable on capitalising the life interest and inform the spouse or civil partner.

38.1.3 Explain the inheritance tax consequences of capitalising the life interest.

38.1.4 If the issue are of full age and capacity, they and the spouse or civil partner can, under the rule in *Saunders* v. *Vautier,* agree to bring the settlement to an end and divide up the assets on any basis they wish. Therefore, if applicable, inform them of this and explain the inheritance tax consequences.

Note:

(i) See *Saunders* v. *Vautier* (1841) EWHC Ch J82.

38.2 Assets held on statutory trusts for minors

38.2.1 Explain to the personal representatives that they will continue to hold assets for *minors* until the statutory trusts come to an end.

38.2.2 Provide the personal representatives with a written explanation of:

    (a) the terms of the statutory trusts;

    (b) their obligations to invest the trust funds and produce accounts for the beneficiaries; and

    (c) their powers in relation to capital and income.

38.2.3 Mark the transition from *estate administration* to trusteeship with an assent or written appropriation.

PART D

ADVISING ON VARIATION OF DISPOSITIONS

39   TAKING INSTRUCTIONS ON VARIATION OF DISPOSITIONS

39.1   When acting for the personal representatives, make clear to them that the standard retainer for the *administration of an estate* does not include the provision of advice on variation of dispositions.

39.2   When acting as personal representatives, make clear to beneficiaries that the provision of advice on variation of dispositions is not part of the duties of a personal representative.

39.3   If it appears appropriate to inform personal representatives and/or beneficiaries that a post-death variation may have advantages for them, for example, by achieving a tax savings:

    (a)   explain in outline the advantages and ask whether they want detailed advice; and

    (b)   if they do want detailed advice:

         (i)   explain that they are not required to instruct you but can go elsewhere; and

         (ii)   provide clear information in writing on the basis on which you would charge.

40   WHEN INSTRUCTED ON VARIATION OF DISPOSITIONS

40.1   Provide advice to help beneficiaries to make decisions which are in their best interests.

40.2   Prepare any necessary documentation in a timely manner.

40.3   In the case of variations in favour of charities:

    (a)   inform the charity of the variation; and

    (b)   obtain confirmation from the charity that it has been informed.

40.4   Submit documentation to HM Revenue and Customs.

PART E

CLAIMS UNDER THE INHERITANCE (PROVISION FOR FAMILY AND DEPENDANTS) ACT 1975

41   ACTION REQUIRED WHERE A CLAIM IS MADE

41.1   Where you are acting in the *administration of an estate* and a claim under the Inheritance (Provision for Family and Dependants) Act 1975 is made or it seems likely that one will be made:

(a)   inform the beneficiaries;

(b)   explain the process for a claim and the effect on the *administration of the estate*;

(c)   consider whether any third parties need to be informed of the probable delay in completing the administration;

(d)   consider whether the probable delay in completing the administration requires you to take any additional steps in relation to protecting assets and/or investing available funds.

42   ACTING FOR PERSONAL REPRESENTATIVES WHERE A CLAIM IS MADE

42.1   A claim under the Inheritance (Provision for Family and Dependants) Act 1975 is not a claim against the estate so advise the personal representatives to remain neutral and await the outcome of the litigation.

42.2   If the personal representatives are remaining neutral, state this in the acknowledgement of service.

42.3   Prepare a witness statement for the personal representatives providing the information required by the Civil Procedure Rules, rule 57.16.5 and Practice Direction 57, para.16.

42.4   If personal representatives who are also beneficiaries wish to defend the claim, explain that they are free to do so but must not neglect the tasks required of the personal representatives.

42.5   Be aware that, if the *practice* has the necessary expertise, it can act for personal representatives who are defending a claim under the Inheritance (Provision for Family and Dependants) Act 1975 in their capacity as beneficiaries. There should be no conflicts of interests or risk of breach of confidentiality since all information about the value and assets/liabilities will be made known to the claimant in the Part 57 Witness Statement. However, consider whether acting in both capacities is in the best interests of the defendant(s) or whether it would be preferable to refer them to another *practice*.

42.6   If the *practice* has the necessary expertise, it can normally act for personal representatives who are bringing a claim provided they bring no claim which is adverse to the estate. However, consider whether acting in both capacities is in the best interests of the claimant(s) or whether it would be preferable to refer them to another *practice*.

42.7   If a personal representative proposes to bring other claims which are adverse to the estate, advise that this is in conflict with his/her fiduciary duties to the estate.

42.8   If the personal representative continues with the adverse action, advise any other personal representatives or, if none, the residuary beneficiaries of the estate, to apply for the removal of the claimant as personal representative under the Administration of Justice Act 1985, s.50.

PART F

GENERAL PRACTICE POLICIES

GP.1   CLIENTS WITH A DISABILITY

A *practice* will have a written policy to help prevent unlawful discrimination in relation to the provision of services to *clients* with a disability. This policy will address the following matters:

(1) Enquiries to be made before an interview as to whether the *client* has any visual, communication or mobility problems.

(2) Adjustments it is reasonable for the *practice* to make. These are likely to include:

    (a) provision of large print or Braille correspondence and documents at no cost;

    (b) arrangements for access and parking suitable for less mobile *clients*;

    (c) visits to the *client* to take instructions instead of requiring the *client* to come to the office.

(3) Contacts with organisations which can provide trained signers to interpret for *clients* who use sign language and who do not wish to use family members or close friends.

Notes:

(i)   It is not permissible to charge for reasonable adjustments.

(ii)   See the Law Society's Equality and Diversity Requirements: SRA Handbook Practice Note.

(iii)   See the Law Society's Equality Act 2010 Practice Note.

GP.2 ADVICE REQUIRED WHICH THE PRACTICE CANNOT PROVIDE

A *practice* will have a written policy to ensure that *clients* receive appropriate advice and a competent service. This policy will address the following matters:

(1) Those providing services to *clients* must always consider whether the *client* requires advice on a particular matter which is beyond the expertise of the *practice*.

(2) Where this is the case, the *practice* must:

   (a) advise the *client* to seek separate advice on that matter;

   (b) consider whether the best interests of the *client* may require the whole of the *client's* affairs to be dealt with in the context of that advice and, if this is the case, suggest to the *client* that the *practice* ceases to act.

(3) Where a *client* refuses to take separate advice, the *practice* must provide the *client* with a written record of:

   (a) all the general advice given, and in particular any risks identified;

   (b) any offer of detailed advice and whether the offer was accepted or refused;

   (c) the *client's* refusal to follow detailed advice given;

and preserve a copy of the record as part of the file.

PART G

WILL DRAFTING PRACTICE POLICIES

WP.1   TAKING INSTRUCTIONS

A *practice* will have a written policy to help with the management of risk relating to taking instructions. This policy will address the following matters:

(1)   Whether customer due diligence is to be carried out as a matter of course, even though it is not required under the Money Laundering Regulations 2007 for the making of a will. (This may be considered as a sensible precaution and to prevent delay if a *client* requires advice on matters such as inheritance tax planning which would require customer due diligence.)

(2)   What steps must be taken to check the identity of *clients* to prevent impersonation of a testator/testatrix.

(3)   Whether all instructions are only to be taken face-to-face or whether there are circumstances in which they are accepted in writing and/or online.

(4)   If instructions are accepted in writing and/or online, what additional checks and safeguards are in place to assess potential risks and ensure that the *client* is properly informed.

(5)   The circumstances, if any, when it is acceptable for a will to be written by someone other than the person who took the instructions, the information to be provided to the person drafting the will and the checks to be made to ensure that the will accurately reflects the *client's* instructions.

(6)   Whether *clients* are to be asked to complete a questionnaire before attending a face-to-face interview and, if so, what checks are to be made to establish whether the *client* completed the questionnaire personally or was assisted by a third party.

Note:

(i)   See the Money Laundering Regulations 2007 (SI 2007/2157).

WP.2 RETAINER LETTERS/AGREEMENTS

A *practice* will have a written policy on the use of standard letters/ agreements which set out the terms of the *will drafting* retainer. This policy will address the following:

(1) Matters on which advice will be offered as part of the standard retainer.

(2) Matters outside the standard retainer on which advice can be offered for a separate charge.

(3) Any matters normally falling within a standard *will drafting* retainer which the *practice* is expressly excluding and on which separate advice would, therefore, have to be obtained.

(4) A fee structure clearly showing how charges are made for separate elements of the retainer.

WP.3 CLIENT INFORMATION ON RISK

A *practice* will have a written policy on how the key risks and benefits associated with making a will are communicated to *clients*. This policy will include details on how the *practice* will deal with the following key matters:

(1) Whether the *practice* will have templates for information on risk to be given to *clients*, responsibility for reviewing the content of the templates and ensuring the templates are used correctly.

(2) Communication to the *client* of the message that making a will is not a 'once and for all' activity. There is a risk that a will may cease to carry out the *client's* wishes if circumstances change and so it is therefore desirable to review a will periodically and when significant events occur (particularly births, deaths and decisions to marry, divorce, form or dissolve *UK civil partnerships*).

(3) Advice for *clients* that where a will is stored by another person there is a risk of:

(a) loss or damage; or

(b) disclosure of confidential information;

unless the person storing has appropriate safeguards in place.

(4) A warning to *clients* that a person appointed as a sole executor has wide powers to access and deal with the deceased's assets.

(5) Advising a *client* considering paying the cost of future *estate administration* services at the time of making a will that this may not be in his/her best interests as:

>   **(a)**   the provider may no longer be operating; and
>
>   **(b)**   the agreement may prevent more suitable arrangements being made in light of circumstances.

WP.4   URGENT INSTRUCTIONS

A *practice* will have a written policy setting out how it will deal with the additional risks presented by taking urgent instructions to make a will. This policy will address the following matters:

(1)   The circumstances in which the *practice* will accept such instructions.

(2)   Where such instructions have been accepted, or where a *client's* health suddenly deteriorates, the steps to be taken to try to establish whether:

>   **(a)**   the *client* has testamentary capacity when giving instructions;
>
>   **(b)**   the *client* continues to have capacity at the time the will is executed or, while lacking full capacity, remembers giving instructions and understands that the will has been prepared in accordance with those earlier instructions;
>
>   **(c)**   at the time the will is executed the *client* knows and approves the contents of the will or understands that the will has been prepared in accordance with those earlier instructions; and
>
>   **(d)**   the *client* is acting as a result of undue influence.

(3)   Modifications to the *practice's* normal terms of retainer to reflect the need for urgent action.

(4)   The checklist and template documents to be used when taking such instructions, for example severance of a beneficial joint tenancy, attestation clause for use where the will is signed on behalf of testator/testatrix.

(5)   Circumstances in which it may be appropriate to prepare a codicil to an existing will rather than a new will.

WP.5   CONSISTENCY

A *practice* will have a written policy to help to ensure the consistency and quality of all wills produced by the *practice*. This policy will address the following matters:

(1)   The precedents and/or *will drafting* packages to be generally used by those preparing wills within the *practice* and procedures for periodic review of the suitability of these precedents and packages.

(2)   Where non-standard precedents are used and amended, a copy of the original precedent to be kept with the file in case of later problems.

(3)   Training for those using precedents to ensure that they understand their meaning and purpose.

(4)   Restrictions on those allowed to prepare wills within the *practice* to ensure that only those with an appropriate level of expertise do so.

(5)   Templates for recording instructions for wills.

(6)   Time limits within which key tasks are to be completed.

(7)   Processes in place to evaluate the skill and experience of all those taking instructions for, and drafting, wills to ensure that work is appropriately allocated and completed.

WP.6   ATTENDANCE NOTES

A *practice* will have a written policy setting out how it will ensure that full attendance notes of key meetings are made. This policy will address the use of templates to make attendance notes of meetings at which:

(1)   instructions for wills are given;

(2)   the meaning and effect of wills prepared for the *client* are explained or discussed; and

(3)   wills are executed.

WP.7   GIFTS TO THOSE DRAFTING WILLS OR PERSONS CONNECTED WITH THEM

A *practice* will have a written policy setting out how it will deal with the significant professional conduct issues arising from gifts and legacies to those drafting wills or persons connected with them. This policy will address the following matters:

(1)   A requirement that if a *client* proposes to make a gift, which is of more than a token amount, whether by will or by lifetime gift to:

(a)   the *will drafter*;

(b)   an employee, partner, director or owner of the *practice* to which the *will drafter* belongs;

(c)   a family member of the above;

the *will drafter* must normally refuse to act until:

(i)   the *client* has obtained independent legal advice; and

(ii) the *will drafter* has received written confirmation from the independent adviser that such advice has been obtained.

(2) A limited exception to the requirement for independent legal advice where:

(a) the *client* is a member of the beneficiary's family; and

(b) the amount being given to the beneficiary is not disproportionate, taking into account the reasonable expectations of others who would reasonably expect to benefit because of their relationship to the deceased.

(3) A requirement that even where instructions fall within the limited exception:

(a) the *will drafter* should obtain permission to act from a designated *practice* member or members; or

(b) if the *will drafter* is the sole owner of the business, the *will drafter* should consider whether it is appropriate to act; and

(c) those deciding whether or not it is appropriate to act should consider the need to avoid conflict of interests and act in the best interests of the *client*.

WP.8 STORAGE OF WILLS AND RETENTION OF FILES

A *practice* will have a written policy for dealing with the safe storage of wills and the retention of files. This policy will address the following matters:

(1) Whether a charge is to be made for storage of wills.

(2) Appropriate systems to allow for the efficient identification and retrieval of stored wills.

(3) An appropriate system, in relation to wills made by the *practice* after this policy is put in place, to identify wills appointing members of the *practice* as executors and/or trustees and an agreed policy on the steps to be taken to inform *clients* if such persons die or leave the *practice*.

(4) An appropriate system, in relation to wills made by the *practice* before this policy is put in place, to take effect when a member of the *practice* leaves to identify wills appointing that person as executor and/or trustee and an agreed procedure on the steps to be taken to inform *clients* if such persons die or leave the *practice*.

(5) Guidelines on who can access wills and will files.

(6) Appropriate storage arrangements to ensure physical security of wills and will files.

(7) Guidelines on the length of period for which wills and will files are to be retained.

Note:

(i)   See the Law Society's File Retention: Wills and Probate Practice Note.

PART H

ESTATE ADMINISTRATION PRACTICE POLICIES

EP.1   ESTATE ADMINISTRATION RETAINER LETTERS/AGREEMENTS

A *practice* will have a written policy on its use of standard letters/agreements setting out the terms of the *estate administration* retainer. This policy will address the following:

(1)   Matters which are included as part of the standard *estate administration* retainer.

(2)   Matters outside the standard *estate administration* retainer on which advice can be offered for a separate charge.

(3)   Any matters normally falling within a standard *estate administration* retainer which the *practice* is expressly excluding and on which separate advice would, therefore, have to be obtained.

(4)   Fee structure showing clearly how charges are made and whether a separate charge is made for acting as executor and/or trustee as opposed to dealing with the work involved and whether charges are calculated on a time basis and/or include a value element.

(5)   Explanation of the *practice's* obligations in relation to anti-money laundering and the proceeds of crime.

(6)   Warning that payments to the beneficiaries of the estate will be made by cheque or bank transfer to the person entitled and not to third parties unless there is a clear reason for payment to the third party.

EP.2   RENUNCIATION OF EXECUTORSHIP AND TRUSTEESHIP AT THE REQUEST OF THOSE ENTITLED TO THE ESTATE

A *practice* will have a written policy to set out the way in which it deals with requests for renunciation of executorship and trusteeship. This policy will deal with the following matters:

(1)   A requirement that such requests are to be considered in light of the reasons for the original appointment.

(2)   If the reasons for the original appointment continue to operate, it is inappropriate to renounce. Examples of situations where renunciation would not be appropriate are where the testator/testatrix:

    (a)   was concerned about tensions between family members and expressed a wish for an impartial professional to act, and those tensions continue to exist; or

    (b)   was concerned about the complexity of the estate and wished to spare family members the responsibility of dealing with those complexities, and those complexities remain; or

    (c)   did not consider that family members were mature enough to deal with the estate, and this remains the case.

(3)   Where circumstances have changed since the appointment, renunciation may be appropriate. Examples of changes which might justify renunciation are:

    (a)   the tensions that caused the testator/testatrix concern no longer exist, perhaps because certain beneficiaries have died; or

    (b)   the estate is significantly less complex than it was at the date the will was made; or

    (c)   family members are significantly more mature than they were at the date the will was made.

(4)   Where members of the *practice* are appointed as both executors and trustees, it is necessary to consider separately whether it is appropriate to disclaim the trusteeship as well as renouncing the executorship, as the two roles are different.

(5)   Giving written acknowledgements of receipt of such requests, which include a time frame for giving a substantive reply.

(6)   A time frame for acknowledging such requests and for giving a substantive reply which properly reflects the need for promptness, (for example, five working days for an acknowledgement and a further 10 working days for a substantive reply).

Note:

(i)   Where there is no request, a *practice* is free to take its own decision to renounce having considered the nature and size of the estate.

EP.3   **CONSISTENCY IN ESTATE ADMINISTRATION**

A *practice* will have a written policy to ensure the consistency and quality of its *estate administration* work. This policy will address the following matters:

(1)   The precedents and/or *estate administration* packages to be used by those dealing with *estate administration* within the *practice* and procedures for the periodic review of the suitability of these precedents and packages.

(2)   Training for those using such precedents and packages to ensure that they understand their meaning and purpose.

(3)   Processes in place to evaluate the skill and experience of all those dealing with *estate administration* to ensure that work is appropriately allocated and completed.

(4)   Time limits within which tasks to be completed.

(5)   Supervision and internal controls to ensure that all *client* money is properly handled and that all assets are properly accounted for.

(6)   Frequency of communication with personal representatives or residuary beneficiaries unless varied by agreement.

PART I

RECOMMENDED FURTHER READING

LAW SOCIETY PUBLICATIONS

Angus, T., Clarke, A., Hewitt, P. and Reed, P. (2006) *Inheritance Act Claims: A practical guide*. The Law Society.

Bielanska C., Terrell, M. and Ashton, G. (eds) (2010) *Elderly Client Handbook* 4th edition. The Law Society, in association with Solicitors for the Elderly.

British Medical Association and the Law Society (2009) *Assessment of Mental Capacity: a practical guide for doctors and lawyers* 3rd edition. The Law Society.

King, L. (ed) (2010) *Probate Practitioner's Handbook* 6th edition. The Law Society.

Law Society's Private Client Section and the Institute of Legacy Management (2012) *Charities as Beneficiaries* 3rd edition. The Law Society.

Riddett, R., King, L. and Gausden P. (2012) *Will Draftsman's Handbook* 9th edition. The Law Society.

Steel, G. (2012) *Trust Practitioner's Handbook* 3rd edition. The Law Society.

Ward, C. (2011) *Lasting Powers of Attorney: A practical guide* 2nd edition. The Law Society.

Administration of Estates Act 1925 extracts

PART 3 – ADMINISTRATION OF ASSETS

33 Trust for sale

(1)   On the death of a person intestate as to any real or personal estate, that estate shall be held in trust by his personal representatives with the power to sell it.

(2)   The personal representatives shall pay out of–

   (a)   the ready money of the deceased (so far as not disposed of by his will, if any); and
   (b)   any not money arising from disposing of any other part of his estate (after payment of costs),

   all such funeral, testamentary and administration expenses, debts and other liabilities as are properly payable thereout having regard to the rules of administration contained in this Part of this Act, and out of the residue of the said money the personal representative shall set aside a fund sufficient to provide for any pecuniary legacies bequeathed by the will (if any) of the deceased.

(3)   During the minority of any beneficiary or the subsistence of any life interest and pending the distribution of the whole or any part of the estate of the deceased, the personal representatives may invest the residue of the said money, or so much thereof as may not have been distributed, under the Trustee Act 2000.

(4)   The residue of the said money and any investments for the time being representing the same, and any part of the estate of the deceased which remains unsold and is not required for the administration purposes aforesaid, is in this Act referred to as 'the residuary estate of the intestate.'

(5)   The income (including net rents and profits of real estate and chattels real after payment of rates, taxes, rent, costs of insurance, repairs and other outgoings properly attributable to income) of so much of the real and personal estate of the deceased as may not be disposed of by his will, if any, or may not be required for the administration purposes aforesaid, may, however such estate is invested, as from the death of the deceased, be treated and applied as income, and for that purpose any necessary apportionment may be made between tenant for life and remainderman.

(6)   Nothing in this section affects the rights of any creditor of the deceased or the rights of the Crown in respect of death duties.

(7)   Where the deceased leaves a will, this section has effect subject to the provisions contained in the will.

PART 4 – DISTRIBUTION OF RESIDUARY ESTATE

46 Succession to real and personal estate on intestacy

(1)   The residuary estate of an intestate shall be distributed in the manner or be held on the trusts mentioned in this section, namely:–

(i)   If the intestate leaves a spouse or civil partner, then in accordance with the following table:

If the intestate–
(1) leaves–
    (a) no issue, and
    (b) no parent, or brother or sister of the whole blood, or issue of a brother or sister of the whole blood.
	the residuary estate shall be held in trust for the surviving spouse or civil partner absolutely.

(2) leaves issue (whether or not persons mentioned in sub-paragraph (b) above also survive).	the surviving spouse or civil partner shall take the personal chattels absolutely and, in addition, the residuary estate of the intestate (other than the personal chattels) shall stand charged with the payment of a fixed net sum, free of death duties and costs, to the surviving spouse or civil partner with interest thereon from the date of the death at such rate as the Lord Chancellor may specify by order until paid or appropriated, and, subject to providing for that sum and the interest thereon, the residuary estate (other than the personal chattels) shall be held– (a) as to one half upon trust for the surviving spouse or civil partner during his or her life, and, subject to such life interest, on the statutory trusts for the issue of the intestate, and (b) as to the other half, on the statutory trusts for the issue of the intestate.

(3) leaves one or more of the following, that is to say, a parent, a brother or sister of the whole blood, or issue of a brother or sister of the whole blood, but leaves no issue.	the surviving spouse or civil partner shall take the personal chattels absolutely and, in addition, the residuary estate of the intestate (other than the personal chattels) shall stand charged with the payment of a fixed net sum, free of death duties and costs, to the surviving spouse or civil partner with interest thereon from the date of the death at such rate as the Lord Chancellor may specify by order until paid or appropriated, and, subject to providing for that sum and the interest thereon, the residuary estate (other than the personal chattels) shall be held– (a) as to one half in trust for the surviving spouse or civil partner absolutely, and (b) as to the other half– (i) where the intestate leaves one parent or both parents (whether or not brothers or sisters of the intestate or their issue also survive) in trust for the parent absolutely or, as the case may be, for the two parents in equal shares absolutely, (ii) where the intestate leaves no parent, on the statutory trusts for the brothers and sisters of the whole blood of the intestate.

The fixed net sums referred to in paragraphs (2) and (3) of this Table shall be of the amounts provided by or under section 1 of the Family Provision Act 1966.

(ii) If the intestate leaves issue but no spouse or civil partner, the residuary estate of the intestate shall be held on the statutory trusts for the issue of the intestate;

(iii) If the intestate leaves no spouse or civil partner and no issue but both parents, then, the residuary estate of the intestate shall be held in trust for the father and mother in equal shares absolutely;

(iv) If the intestate leaves no spouse or civil partner and no issue but one parent, then, the residuary estate of the intestate shall be held in trust for the surviving father or mother absolutely;

(v) If the intestate leaves no spouse or civil partner and no issue and no parent, then the residuary estate of the intestate shall be held in trust for the following persons living at the death of the intestate, and in the following order and manner, namely:–

First, on the statutory trusts for the brothers and sisters of the whole blood of the intestate; but if no person takes an absolutely vested interest under such trusts, then

Secondly, on the statutory trusts for the brothers and sisters of the half blood of the intestate; but if no person takes an absolutely vested interest under such trusts; then

Thirdly, for the grandparents of the intestate and, if more than one survive the intestate, in equal shares; but if there is no member of this class; then

Fourthly, on the statutory trusts for the uncles and aunts of the intestate (being brothers or sisters of the whole blood of a parent of the intestate); but if no person takes an absolutely vested interest under such trusts; then

Fifthly, on the statutory trusts for the uncles and aunts of the intestate (being brothers or sisters of the half blood of a parent of the intestate);

(vi) In default of any person taking an absolute interest under the foregoing provisions, the residuary estate of the intestate shall belong to the Crown or to the Duchy of Lancaster or to the Duke of Cornwall for the time being, as the case may be, as bona vacantia, and in lieu of any right to escheat.

The Crown or the said Duchy or the said Duke may (without prejudice to the powers reserved by section nine of the Civil List Act, 1910, or any other powers), out of the whole or any part of the property devolving on them respectively, provide, in accordance with the existing practice, for dependants, whether kindred or not, of the intestate, and other persons for whom the intestate might reasonably have been expected to make provision.

(1A) The power to make orders under subsection (1) above shall be exercisable by statutory instrument subject to annulment in pursuance of a resolution of either House of Parliament; and any such order may be varied or revoked by a subsequent order made under the power.

(2) A husband and wife shall for all purposes of distribution or division under the foregoing provisions of this section be treated as two persons.

(2A) Where the intestate's spouse or civil partner survived the intestate but died before the end of the period of 28 days beginning with the day on which the intestate died, this section shall have effect as respects the intestate as if the spouse or civil partner had not survived the intestate.

(3) Where the intestate and the intestate's spouse or civil partner have died in circumstances rendering in uncertain which of them survived the other and the intestate's spouse or civil partner is by virtue of section one hundred and eighty-four of the Law of Property Act, 1925, deemed to have survived the intestate, this section shall, nevertheless, have effect as respects the intestate as if the spouse or civil partner had not survived the intestate.

(4) The interest payable on the fixed net sum payable to a surviving spouse or civil partner shall be primarily payable out of income.

46A   Disclaimer or forfeiture on intestacy

(1) This section applies where a person–

(a) is entitled in accordance with section 46 to an interest in the residuary estate of an intestate but disclaims it, or

(b) would have been so entitled had the person not been precluded by the forfeiture rule from acquiring it.

(2)   The person is to be treated for the purposes of this Part as having died immediately before the intestate.

(3)   But in a case within subsection (1)(b), subsection (2) does not affect the power conferred by section 2 of the Forfeiture Act 1982 (power of court to modify the forfeiture rule).

(4)   In this section 'forfeiture rule' has the same meaning as in the Forfeiture Act 1982.

47   Statutory trusts in favour of issue and other classes of relatives of intestate

(1)   Where under this Part of this Act the residuary estate of an intestate, or any part thereof, is directed to be held on the statutory trusts for the issue of the intestate, the same shall be held upon the following trusts, namely:–

   (i)   In trust, in equal shares if more than one, for all or any the children or child of the intestate, living at the death of the intestate, who attain the age of eighteen years or marry under that age or form a civil partnership under that age, and for all or any of the issue living at the death of the intestate who attain the age of eighteen years or marry, or form a civil partnership, under that age of any child of the intestate who predeceases the intestate, such issue to take through all degrees, according to their stocks, in equal shares if more than one, the share which their parent would have taken if living at the death of the intestate, and so that (subject to section 46A) no issue shall take whose parent is living at the death of the intestate and so capable of taking;

   (ii)   The statutory power of advancement, and the statutory provisions which relate to maintenance and accumulation of surplus income, shall apply, but when an infant marries, or forms a civil partnership, such infant shall be entitled to give valid receipts for the income of the infant's share or interest;

   (iii) [*repealed*]

   (iv)   The personal representatives may permit any infant contingently interested to have the use and enjoyment of any personal chattels in such manner and subject to such conditions (if any) as the personal representatives may consider reasonable, and without being liable to account for any consequential loss.

(2)   If the trusts in favour of the issue of the intestate fail by reason of no child or other issue attaining an absolutely vested interest–

   (a)   the residuary estate of the intestate and the income thereof and all statutory accumulations, if any, of the income thereof, or so much thereof as may not have been paid or applied under any power affecting the same, shall go, devolve and be held under the provisions of this Part of this Act as if the intestate had died without leaving issue living at the death of the intestate;

   (b)   references in this Part of this Act to the intestate 'leaving no issue' shall be construed as 'leaving no issue who attain an absolutely vested interest';

   (c)   references in this Part of this Act to the intestate 'leaving issue' or 'leaving a child or other issue' shall be construed as 'leaving issue who attain an absolutely vested interest.'

(3)   Where under this Part of this Act the residuary estate of an intestate or any part thereof is directed to be held on the statutory trusts for any class of relatives of the intestate, other than issue of the intestate, the same shall be held on trusts corresponding to the statutory trusts for the issue of the intestate (other than the provision for bringing any money or property into account) as if such trusts (other than as aforesaid) were repeated with the substitution of references to the members or member of that class for references to the children or child of the intestate.

(4)   References in paragraph (i) of subsection (1) of the last foregoing section to the intestate

leaving, or not leaving, a member of the class consisting of brothers or sisters of the whole blood of the intestate and issue of brothers or sisters of the whole blood of the intestate shall be construed as references to the intestate leaving, or not leaving, a member of that class who attains an absolutely vested interest.

(4A) Subsections (2) and (4) are subject to section 46A.

(4B) Subsections (4C) and (4D) apply if a beneficiary under the statutory trusts–

  (a) fails to attain an absolutely vested interest because the beneficiary dies without having reached 18 and without having married or formed a civil partnership, and

  (b) dies leaving issue.

(4C) The beneficiary is to be treated for the purposes of this Part as having died immediately before the intestate.

(4D) The residuary estate (together with the income from it and any statutory accumulations of income from it) or so much of it as has not been paid or applied under a power affecting it is to devolve accordingly.

47A Right of surviving spouse to have own life interest redeemed

(1) Where a surviving spouse or civil partner is entitled to a life interest in part of the residuary estate, and so elects, the personal representative shall purchase or redeem the life interest by paying the capital value thereof to the tenant for life, or the persons deriving title under the tenant for life, and the costs of the transaction; and thereupon the residuary estate of the intestate may be dealt with and distributed free from the life interest.

(2) [repealed]

(3) An election under this section shall only be exercisable if at the time of the election the whole of the said part of the residuary estate consists of property in possession, but, for the purposes of this section, a life interest in property partly in possession and partly not in possession may be treated as consisting of two separate life interests in those respective parts of the property.

(3A) The capital value shall be reckoned in such manner as the Lord Chancellor may by order direct, and an order under this subsection may include transitional provisions.

(3B) The power to make orders under subsection (3A) above shall be exercisable by statutory instrument subject to annulment in pursuance of a resolution of either House of Parliament; and any such order may be varied or revoked by a subsequent order made under the power.

(4) [repealed]

(5) An election under this section shall be exercisable only within the period of twelve months from the date on which representation with respect to the estate of the intestate is first taken out:

Provided that if the surviving spouse or civil partner satisfies the court that the limitation to the said period of twelve months will operate unfairly–

  (a) in consequence of the representation first taken out being probate of a will subsequently revoked on the ground that the will was invalid or,

  (b) in consequence of a question whether a person had an interest in the estate, or as to the nature of an interest in the estate, not having been determined at the time when representation was first taken out, or

  (c) in consequence of some other circumstances affecting the administration or distribution of the estate,

the court may extend the said period.

(6) An election under this section shall be exercisable, except where the tenant for life is the

sole personal representative, by notifying the personal representative (or, where there are two or more personal representatives of whom one is the tenant for life all of them except the tenant for life) in writing; and a notification in writing under this subsection shall not be revocable except with the consent of the personal representative.

(7)   Where the tenant for life is the sole personal representative an election under this section shall not be effective unless written notice thereof is given to the Senior Registrar of the Family Division of the High Court within the period within which it must be made; and provision may be made by probate rules for keeping a record of such notices and making that record available to the public.

In this subsection the expression 'probate rules' means rules of court made under section 127 of the Supreme Court Act 1981.

(8)   An election under this section by a tenant for life who is an infant shall be as valid and binding as it would be if the tenant for life were of age; but the personal representative shall, instead of paying the capital value of the life interest to the tenant for life, deal with it in the same manner as with any other part of the residuary estate to which the tenant for life is absolutely entitled.

(9)   In considering for the purposes of the foregoing provisions of this section the question when representation was first taken out, a grant limited to settled land or to trust property shall be left out of account and a grant limited to real estate or to personal estate shall be left out of account unless a grant limited to the remainder of the estate has previously been made or is made at the same time.

PART 5 – SUPPLEMENTAL

55   Definitions

In this Act, unless the context otherwise requires, the following expressions have the meanings hereby assigned to them respectively, that is to say:–

(1)   (i)   'Administration' means, with reference to the real and personal estate of a deceased person, letters of administration, whether general or limited, or with the will annexed or otherwise:

        (ii)   'Administrator' means a person to whom administration is granted:

        (iii)   'Conveyance' includes a mortgage, charge by way of legal mortgage, lease, assent, vesting, declaration, vesting instrument, disclaimer, release and every other assurance of property or of an interest therein by any instrument, except a will, and 'convey' has a corresponding meaning, and 'disposition' includes a 'conveyance' also a devise bequest and an appointment of property contained in a will, and 'dispose of' has a corresponding meaning:

        (iiiA) 'the County Court limit', in relation to any enactment contained in this Act, means the amount for the time being specified by an Order in Council under section 145 of the County Courts Act 1984 as the county court limit for the purposes of that enactment (or, where no such Order in Council has been made, the corresponding limit specified by Order in Council under section 192 of the County Courts Act 1959);

        (iv)   'the Court' means the High Court, and also the county court, where that court has jurisdiction,

        (v)   'Income' includes rents and profits:

        (vi)   'Intestate' includes a person who leaves a will but dies intestate as to some beneficial interest in his real or personal estate:

        (via) 'Land' has the same meaning as in the Law of Property Act 1925.

        (vii) 'Legal estates' means the estates charges and interests in or over land (subsisting

91

or created at law) which are by statute authorised to subsist or to be created at law; and 'equitable interests' means all other interests and charges in or over land.

(viii) [*repealed*]

(ix) 'Pecuniary legacy' includes an annuity, a general legacy, a demonstrative legacy so far as it is not discharged out of the designated property, and any other general direction by a testator for the payment of money, including all death duties free from which any devise, bequest, or payment is made to take effect:

(x) 'Personal chattels' mean carriages, horses, stable furniture and effects (not used for business purposes), motor cars and accessories (not used for business purposes), garden effects, domestic animals, plate, plated articles, linen, china, glass, books, pictures, prints, furniture, jewellery, articles of household or personal use or ornament, musical and scientific instruments and apparatus, wines, liquors and consumable stores, but do not include any chattels used at the death of the intestate for business purposes nor money or securities for money:

(xi) 'Personal representative' means the executor, original or by representation, or administrator for the time being of a deceased person, and as regards any liability for the payment of death duties includes any person who takes possession of or intermeddles with the property of a deceased person without the authority of the personal representatives or the court, and 'executor' includes a person deemed to be appointed executor as respects settled land:

(xii) 'Possession' includes the receipt of rents and profits or the right to receive the same, if any:

(xiii) 'Prescribed' means prescribed by rules of court

(xiv) 'Probate' means the probate of a will:

(xv) [*repealed*]

(xvi) [*repealed*]

(xvii) 'Property' includes a thing in action and any interest in real or personal property:

(xviii) 'Purchaser' means a lessee, mortgagee or other person who in good faith acquires an interest in property for valuable consideration, also an intending purchaser and 'valuable consideration' includes marriage, and formation of a civil partnership, but does not include a nominal consideration in money:

(xix) 'Real estate' save as provided in Part IV of this Act means real estate, including chattels real, which by virtue of Part I of this Act devolves on the personal representative of a deceased person:

(xx) 'Representation' means the probate of a will and administration, and the expression 'taking out representation' refers to the obtaining of the probate of a will or of the grant of administration:

(xxi) 'Rent' includes a rent service or a rentcharge, or other rent, toll, duty, or annual or periodical payment in money or money's worth, issuing out of or charged upon land, but does not include mortgage interest; and 'rentcharge' includes a fee farm rent:

(xxii) [*repealed*]

(xxiii) 'Securities' include stocks, funds, or shares:

(xxiv) 'Tenant for life,' 'statutory owner,' . . . 'settled land,' 'settlement,' 'trustees of the settlement,' 'term of years absolute,' 'death duties,' and 'legal mortgage' have the same meanings as in the Settled Land Act 1925, and 'entitled interest' and 'charge by way of legal mortgage' have the same meanings as in the Law of Property Act 1925:

(xxv) 'Treasury solicitor' means the solicitor for the affairs of His Majesty's Treasury, and includes the solicitor for the affairs of the Duchy of Lancaster:

(xxvi) 'Trust corporation' means the public trustee or a corporation either appointed by the court in any particular case to be a trustee or entitled by rules made under subsection (3) of section four of the Public Trustee Act, 1906, to act as custodian trustee:

(xxvii) [*repealed*]

(xxviii)'Will' includes codicil.

(2) References to a child or issue living at the death of any person include a child or issue en ventre sa mère at the death.

(3) References to the estate of a deceased person include property over which the deceased exercises a general power of appointment (including the statutory power to dispose of entailed interests) by his will.

APPENDIX A2

Children Act 1989, ss.3 and 5

PART 1 – INTRODUCTORY

3   Meaning of 'parental responsibility'

(1)   In this Act 'parental responsibility' means all the rights, duties, powers, responsibilities and authority which by law a parent of a child has in relation to the child and his property.

(2)   It also includes the rights, powers and duties which a guardian of the child's estate (appointed, before the commencement of section 5, to act generally) would have had in relation to the child and his property.

(3)   The rights referred to in subsection (2) include, in particular, the right of the guardian to receive or recover in his own name, for the benefit of the child, property of whatever description and wherever situated which the child is entitled to receive or recover.

(4)   The fact that a person has, or does not have, parental responsibility for a child shall not affect–

    (a)   any obligation which he may have in relation to the child (such as a statutory duty to maintain the child); or

    (b)   any rights which, in the event of the child's death, he (or any other person) may have in relation to the child's property.

(5)   A person who–

    (a)   does not have parental responsibility for a particular child; but

    (b)   has care of the child,

may (subject to the provisions of this Act) do what is reasonable in all the circumstances of the case for the purpose of safeguarding or promoting the child's welfare.

5   Appointment of guardians

(1)   Where an application with respect to a child is made to the court by any individual, the court may by order appoint that individual to be the child's guardian if–

    (a)   the child has no parent with parental responsibility for him; or

    (b)   a residence order has been made with respect to the child in favour of a parent, guardian or special guardian of his who has died while the order was in force; or

    (c)   paragraph (b) does not apply, and the child's only or last surviving special guardian dies.

(2)   The power conferred by subsection (1) may also be exercised in any family proceedings if the court considers that the order should be made even though no application has been made for it.

(3)   A parent who has parental responsibility for his child may appoint another individual to be the child's guardian in the event of his death.

(4)   A guardian of a child may appoint another individual to take his place as the child's guardian in the event of his death; and a special guardian of a child may appoint another individual to be the child's guardian in the event of his death

(5)   An appointment under subsection (3) or (4) shall not have effect unless it is made in writing, is dated and is signed by the person making the appointment or–

     (a)   in the case of an appointment made by a will which is not signed by the testator, is signed at the direction of the testator in accordance with the requirements of section 9 of the Wills Act 1837; or

     (b)   in any other case, is signed at the direction of the person making the appointment, in his presence and in the presence of two witnesses who each attest the signature.

(6)   A person appointed as a child's guardian under this section shall have parental responsibility for the child concerned.

(7)   Where–

     (a)   on the death of any person making an appointment under subsection (3) or (4), the child concerned has no parent with parental responsibility for him; or

     (b)   immediately before the death of any person making such an appointment, a residence order in his favour was in force with respect to the child or he was the child's only (or last surviving) special guardian,

the appointment shall take effect on the death of that person.

(8)   Where, on the death of any person making an appointment under subsection (3) or (4)–

     (a)   the child concerned has a parent with parental responsibility for him; and

     (b)   subsection (7)(b) does not apply,

the appointment shall take effect when the child no longer has a parent who has parental responsibility for him.

(9)   Subsections (1) and (7) do not apply if the residence order referred to in paragraph (b) of those subsections was also made in favour of a surviving parent of the child.

(10)   Nothing in this section shall be taken to prevent an appointment under subsection (3) or (4) being made by two or more persons acting jointly.

(11)   Subject to any provision made by rules of court, no court shall exercise the High Court's inherent jurisdiction to appoint a guardian of the estate of any child.

(12)   Where rules of court are made under subsection (11) they may prescribe the circumstances in which, and conditions subject to which, an appointment of such a guardian may be made.

(13)   A guardian of a child may only be appointed in accordance with the provisions of this section.

APPENDIX A3

Civil Partnership Act 2004, s.1

PART 1 – INTRODUCTION

1 Civil partnership

(1)   A civil partnership is a relationship between two people of the same sex ('civil partners')–

   (a)   which is formed when they register as civil partners of each other–

      (i)   in England or Wales (under Part 2),
      (ii)   in Scotland (under Part 3),
      (iii) in Northern Ireland (under Part 4), or
      (iv)   outside the United Kingdom under an Order in Council made under Chapter 1 of Part 5 (registration at British consulates etc. or by armed forces personnel), or

   (b)   which they are treated under Chapter 2 of Part 5 as having formed (at the time determined under that Chapter) by virtue of having registered an overseas relationship.

(2)   Subsection (1) is subject to the provisions of this Act under or by virtue of which a civil partnership is void.

(3)   A civil partnership ends only on death, dissolution or annulment.

(4)   The references in subsection (3) to dissolution and annulment are to dissolution and annulment having effect under or recognised in accordance with this Act.

(5)   References in this Act to an overseas relationship are to be read in accordance with Chapter 2 of Part 5.

Equality Act 2010, s.20

PART 2 – EQUALITY: KEY CONCEPTS

Adjustments for disabled persons

20   Duty to make adjustments

(1)   Where this Act imposes a duty to make reasonable adjustments on a person, this section, sections 21 and 22 and the applicable Schedule apply; and for those purposes, a person on whom the duty is imposed is referred to as A.

(2)   The duty comprises the following three requirements.

(3)   The first requirement is a requirement, where a provision, criterion or practice of A's puts a disabled person at a substantial disadvantage in relation to a relevant matter in comparison with persons who are not disabled, to take such steps as it is reasonable to have to take to avoid the disadvantage.

(4)   The second requirement is a requirement, where a physical feature puts a disabled person at a substantial disadvantage in relation to a relevant matter in comparison with persons who are not disabled, to take such steps as it is reasonable to have to take to avoid the disadvantage.

(5)   The third requirement is a requirement, where a disabled person would, but for the provision of an auxiliary aid, be put at a substantial disadvantage in relation to a relevant matter in comparison with persons who are not disabled, to take such steps as it is reasonable to have to take to provide the auxiliary aid.

(6)   Where the first or third requirement relates to the provision of information, the steps which it is reasonable for A to have to take include steps for ensuring that in the circumstances concerned the information is provided in an accessible format.

(7)   A person (A) who is subject to a duty to make reasonable adjustments is not (subject to express provision to the contrary) entitled to require a disabled person, in relation to whom A is required to comply with the duty, to pay to any extent A's costs of complying with the duty.

(8)   A reference in section 21 or 22 or an applicable Schedule to the first, second or third requirement is to be construed in accordance with this section.

(9)   In relation to the second requirement, a reference in this section or an applicable Schedule to avoiding a substantial disadvantage includes a reference to–

(a)   removing the physical feature in question,

(b)   altering it, or

(c)   providing a reasonable means of avoiding it.

(10) A reference in this section, section 21 or 22 or an applicable Schedule (apart from paragraphs 2 to 4 of Schedule 4) to a physical feature is a reference to–

    (a) a feature arising from the design or construction of a building,
    (b) a feature of an approach to, exit from or access to a building,
    (c) a fixture or fitting, or furniture, furnishings, materials, equipment or other chattels, in or on premises, or
    (d) any other physical element or quality.

(11) A reference in this section, section 21 or 22 or an applicable Schedule to an auxiliary aid includes a reference to an auxiliary service.

(12) A reference in this section or an applicable Schedule to chattels is to be read, in relation to Scotland, as a reference to moveable property.

(13) The applicable Schedule is, in relation to the Part of this Act specified in the first column of the Table, the Schedule specified in the second column.

Part of this Act	Applicable Schedule
Part 3 (services and public functions)	Schedule 2
Part 4 (premises)	Schedule 4
Part 5 (work)	Schedule 8
Part 6 (education)	Schedule 13
Part 7 (associations)	Schedule 15
Each of the Parts mentioned above	Schedule 21

Inheritance Tax Act 1984 extracts

PART 6 – VALUATION

Chapter 3   Sale of shares etc. from deceased's estate

178   Preliminary

(1)   In this Chapter–

'the appropriate person', in relation to any qualifying investments comprised in a person's estate immediately before his death, means the person liable for inheritance tax attributable to the value of those investments or, if there is more than one such person, and one of them is in fact paying the tax, that person;

'the loss on sale' means the amount determined in accordance with section 179(1) below;

'qualifying investments' means (subject to subsection (2) below) shares or securities which are quoted at the date of the death in question holdings in a unit trust which at that date is an authorised unit trust, shares in an open-ended investment company and shares in any common investment fund established under section 42 of the Administration of Justice Act 1982;

'relevant proportion', in relation to the investments to which a claim relates, or any of them, means the proportion by which the loss on sale is reduced under section 180 below;

'sale value', in relation to any qualifying investments, means their value for the purposes of section 179(1)(b) below;

'value on death', in relation to any qualifying investments, means their value for the purposes of section 179(1)(a) below.

(2)   Shares or securities which are comprised in a person's estate immediately before his death and in respect of which listing on a recognised stock exchange or dealing on the Unlisted Securities Market is suspended at that time shall be qualifying investments for the purposes of this Chapter if they are again so listed or dealt in they are sold as mentioned in section 179(1) below or exchanged as mentioned in section 184 below.

(3)   Any reference in this Chapter to the investments to which a claim relates is a reference to all the qualifying investments which, on the making of the claim, are taken into account under section 179(1) below in determining the loss on sale.

(4)   For the purposes of this Chapter–

(a)   the personal representatives of the deceased, and

(b)   the trustees of a settlement,

shall each be treated as a single and continuing body of persons (distinct from the persons who may from time to time be the personal representatives or trustees).

(5)   In any case where, for the purposes of this Chapter, it is necessary to determine the price at which any investments were purchased or sold or the best consideration that could reasonably have been obtained on the sale of any investments, no account shall be taken of expenses (whether by way of commission, stamp duty or otherwise) which are incidental to the sale or purchase.

Chapter 4   Sale of land from deceased's estate

190   Preliminary

(1)   In this Chapter–

'the appropriate person', in relation to any interest in land comprised in a person's estate immediately before his death, means the person liable for inheritance tax attributable to the value of that interest or, if there is more than one such person and one of them is in fact paying the tax, that person;

'interest in land' does not include any estate, interest or right by way of mortgage or other security;

'sale price', in relation to any interest in land, means the price for which it is sold or, if greater, the best consideration that could reasonably have been obtained for it at the time of the sale;

'sale value', in relation to any interest in land, means its sale price as increased or reduced under the following provisions of this Chapter;

'value on death', in relation to any interest in land comprised in a person's estate immediately before his death, means the value which, apart from this Chapter, (and apart from section 176 above) would be its value as part of that estate for the purposes of this Act.

(2)   Any reference in this Chapter to the interests to which a claim relates is a reference to the interests to which section 191(1) below applies by virtue of the claim.

(3)   For the purposes of this Chapter—

(a)   the personal representatives of the deceased, and

(b)   the trustees of a settlement,

shall each be treated as a single and continuing body of persons (distinct from the persons who may from time to time be the personal representatives or trustees).

(4)   In any case where, for the purposes of this Chapter, it is necessary to determine the price at which any interest was purchased or sold or the best consideration that could reasonably have been obtained on the sale of any interest, no account shall be taken of expenses (whether by way of commission, stamp duty or stamp duty land tax or otherwise) which are incidental to the sale or purchase.

PART 8 – ADMINISTRATION AND COLLECTION

Payment

230   Acceptance of property in satisfaction of tax

(1)   The Board may, if they think fit and the Secretary of State agrees, on the application of any person liable to pay tax or interest payable under section 233 below, accept in satisfaction of the whole or any part of it any property to which this section applies.

(2)   This section applies to any such land as may be agreed upon between the Board and the person liable to pay tax.

(3)   This section also applies to any objects which are or have been kept in any building–

    (a)   if the Board have determined to accept or have accepted that building in satisfaction or part satisfaction of tax or of estate duty, or

    (b)   if the building or any interest in it belongs to Her Majesty in right of the Crown or of the Duchy of Lancaster, or belongs to the Duchy of Cornwall or belongs to a Government department or is held for the purposes of a Government department, or

    (c)   if the building is one of which the Secretary of State is guardian under the Ancient Monuments and Archaeological Areas Act 1979 or of which the Department of the Environment for Northern Ireland is guardian under the Historic Monuments Act (Northern Ireland) 1971, or

    (d)   if the building belongs to any body within Schedule 3 to this Act,

in any case where it appears to the Secretary of State desirable for the objects to remain associated with the building.

(4)   This section also applies to–

    (a)   any picture, print, book, manuscript, work of art, scientific object or other thing which the Secretary of State is satisfied is pre-eminent for its national, scientific, historic or artistic interest, and

    (b)   any collection or group of pictures, prints, books, manuscripts, works of art, scientific objects or other things if the Secretary of State is satisfied that the collection or group, taken as a whole, is pre-eminent for its national, scientific, historic or artistic interest.

(5)   In this section–

'national interest' includes interest within any part of the United Kingdom;

and in determining under subsection (4) above whether an object or collection or group of objects is pre-eminent, regard shall be had to any significant association of the object, collection or group with a particular place.

(6)   The functions of the Ministers under this section in relation to the acceptance, in satisfaction of tax, of property in which there is a Scottish interest may be exercised separately.

(7)   For the purposes of subsection (6) a Scottish interest in the property exists–

    (a)   where the property is located in Scotland; or

    (b)   the person liable to pay the tax has expressed a wish or imposed a condition on his offer of the property in satisfaction of tax that it be displayed in Scotland or disposed of or transferred to a body or institution in Scotland.

Inheritance (Provision for Family and Dependants) Act 1975

1   Application for financial provision from deceased's estate

(1)   Where after the commencement of this Act a person dies domiciled in England and Wales and is survived by any of the following persons–

(a)   the spouse or civil partner of the deceased;

(b)   a former spouse or former civil partner of the deceased, but not one who has formed a subsequent marriage or civil partnership;

(ba) any person (not being a person included in paragraph (a) or (b) above) to whom subsection (1A) or (1B) below applies;

(c)   a child of the deceased;

(d)   any person (not being a child of the deceased) who, in the case of any marriage or civil partnership to which the deceased was at any time a party, was treated by the deceased as a child of the family in relation to that marriage or civil partnership;

(e)   any person (not being a person included in the foregoing paragraphs of this subsection) who immediately before the death of the deceased was being maintained, either wholly or partly, by the deceased;

that person may apply to the court for an order under section 2 of this Act on the ground that the disposition of the deceased's estate effected by his will or the law relating to intestacy, or the combination of his will and that law, is not such as to make reasonable financial provision for the applicant.

(1A) This subsection applies to a person if the deceased died on or after 1st January 1996 and, during the whole of the period of two years ending immediately before the date when the deceased died, the person was living–

(a)   in the same household as the deceased, and

(b)   as the husband or wife of the deceased.

(1B) This subsection applies to a person if for the whole of the period of two years ending immediately before the date when the deceased died the person was living–

(a)   in the same household as the deceased, and

(b)   as the civil partner of the deceased.

(2)   In this Act 'reasonable financial provision'–

(a)   in the case of an application made by virtue of subsection (1)(a) above by the husband or wife of the deceased (except where, at the date of death, a separation order under the Family Law Act 1996 was in force in relation to the marriage and the separation was continuing), means such financial provision as it would be reasonable in all the circumstances of the case for a husband or wife to receive, whether or not that provision is required for his or her maintenance;

(aa) in the case of an application made by virtue of subsection (1)(a) above by the civil partner of the deceased (except where, at the date of death, a separation order under Chapter 2 of Part 2 of the Civil Partnership Act 2004 was in force in relation to the civil partnership and the separation was continuing), means such financial provision as it would be reasonable in all the circumstances of the case for a civil partner to receive, whether or not that provision is required for his or her maintenance;

(b)   in the case of any other application made by virtue of subsection (1) above, means such financial provision as it would be reasonable in all the circumstances of the case for the applicant to receive for his maintenance.

(3)   For the purposes of subsection (1)(e) above, a person shall be treated as being maintained by the deceased, either wholly or partly, as the case may be, if the deceased, otherwise than for full valuable consideration, was making a substantial contribution in money or money's worth towards the reasonable needs of that person.

2   Powers of court to make orders

(1)   Subject to the provisions of this Act, where an application is made for an order under this section, the court may, if it is satisfied that the disposition of the deceased's estate effected by his will or the law relating to intestacy, or the combination of his will and that law, is not such as to make reasonable financial provision for the applicant, make any one or more of the following orders–

(a)   an order for the making to the applicant out of the net estate of the deceased of such periodical payments and for such term as may be specified in the order;

(b)   an order for the payment to the applicant out of that estate of a lump sum of such amount as may be so specified;

(c)   an order for the transfer to the applicant of such property comprised in that estate as may be so specified;

(d)   an order for the settlement for the benefit of the applicant of such property comprised in that estate as may be so specified;

(e)   an order for the acquisition out of property comprised in that estate of such property as may be so specified and for the transfer of the property so acquired to the applicant or for the settlement thereof for his benefit;

(f)   an order varying any ante-nuptial or post-nuptial settlement (including such a settlement made by will) made on the parties to a marriage to which the deceased was one of the parties, the variation being for the benefit of the surviving party to that marriage, or any child of that marriage, or any person who was treated by the deceased as a child of the family in relation to that marriage;

(g)   an order varying any settlement made–

(i)   during the subsistence of a civil partnership formed by the deceased, or

(ii)   in anticipation of the formation of a civil partnership by the deceased,

on the civil partners (including such a settlement made by will), the variation being for the benefit of the surviving civil partner, or any child of both the civil partners, or any person who was treated by the deceased as a child of the family in relation to that civil partnership.

(2)   An order under subsection (1)(a) above providing for the making out of the net estate of the deceased of periodical payments may provide for–

(a)   payments of such amount as may be specified in the order,

(b)   payments equal to the whole of the income of the net estate or of such portion thereof as may be so specified,

(c)   payments equal to the whole of the income of such part of the net estate as the court may direct to be set aside or appropriated for the making out of the income thereof of payments under this section, or may provide for the amount of the payments or any of them to be determined in any other way the court thinks fit.

(3)   Where an order under subsection (1)(a) above provides for the making of payments of an amount specified in the order, the order may direct that such part of the net estate as may be so specified shall be set aside or appropriated for the making out of the income thereof of those payments; but no larger part of the net estate shall be so set aside or appropriated than is sufficient, at the date of the order, to produce by the income thereof the amount required for the making of those payments.

(4)   An order under this section may contain such consequential and supplemental provisions as the court thinks necessary or expedient for the purpose of giving effect to the order or for the purpose of securing that the order operates fairly as between one beneficiary of the estate of the deceased and another and may, in particular, but without prejudice to the generality of this subsection–

(a)   order any person who holds any property which forms part of the net estate of the deceased to make such payment or transfer such property as may be specified in the order;

(b)   varying the disposition of the deceased's estate effected by the will or the law relating to intestacy, or by both the will and the law relating to intestacy, in such manner as the court thinks fair and reasonable having regard to the provisions of the order and all the circumstances of the case;

(c)   confer on the trustees of any property which is the subject of an order under this section such powers as appear to the court to be necessary or expedient.

3   Matters to which court is to have regard in exercising powers under s 2

(1)   Where an application is made for an order under section 2 of this Act, the court shall, in determining whether the disposition of the deceased's estate effected by his will or the law relating to intestacy, or the combination of his will and that law, is such as to make reasonable financial provision for the applicant and, if the court considers that reasonable financial provision has not been made, in determining whether and in what manner it shall exercise its powers under that section, have regard to the following matters, that is to say–

(a)   the financial resources and financial needs which the applicant has or is likely to have in the foreseeable future;

(b)   the financial resources and financial needs which any other applicant for an order under section 2 of this Act has or is likely to have in the foreseeable future;

(c)   the financial resources and financial needs which any beneficiary of the estate of the deceased has or is likely to have in the foreseeable future;

(d)   any obligations and responsibilities which the deceased had towards any applicant for an order under the said section 2 or towards any beneficiary of the estate of the deceased;

(e)   the size and nature of the net estate of the deceased;

(f)   any physical or mental disability of any applicant for an order under the said section 2 or any beneficiary of the estate of the deceased;

(g)   any other matter, including the conduct of the applicant or any other person, which in the circumstances of the case the court may consider relevant.

(2)   This subsection applies, without prejudice to the generality of paragraph (g) of subsection (1) above, where an application for an order under section 2 of this Act is made by virtue of section 1(1)(a) or (b) of this Act.

The court shall, in addition to the matters specifically mentioned in paragraphs (a) to (f) of that subsection, have regard to–

(a)   the age of the applicant and the duration of the marriage or civil partnership;

(b)   the contribution made by the applicant to the welfare of the family of the deceased, including any contribution made by looking after the home or caring for the family.

In the case of an application by the wife or husband of the deceased, the court shall also, unless at the date of death a separation order under the Family Law Act 1996 was in force and the separation was continuing, have regard to the provision which the applicant might reasonably have expected to receive if on the day on which the deceased died the marriage, instead of being terminated by death, had been terminated by a divorce order.

In the case of an application by the civil partner of the deceased, the court shall also, unless at the date of the death a separation order under Chapter 2 of Part 2 of the Civil Partnership Act 2004 was in force and the separation was continuing, have regard to the provision which the applicant might reasonably have expected to receive if on the day on which the deceased died the civil partnership, instead of being terminated by death, had been terminated by a dissolution order.

(2A)   Without prejudice to the generality of paragraph (g) of subsection (1) above, where an application for an order under section 2 of this Act is made by virtue of section 1(1)(ba) of this Act, the court shall, in addition to the matters specifically mentioned in paragraphs (a) to (f) of that subsection, have regard to–

(a)   the age of the applicant and the length of the period during which the applicant lived as the husband or wife or civil partner of the deceased and in the same household as the deceased;

(b)   the contribution made by the applicant to the welfare of the family of the deceased, including any contribution made by looking after the home or caring for the family.

(3)   Without prejudice to the generality of paragraph (g) of subsection (1) above, where an application for an order under section 2 of this Act is made by virtue of section 1(1)(c) or 1(1)(d) of this Act, the court shall, in addition to the matters specifically mentioned in paragraphs (a) to (f) of that subsection, have regard to the manner in which the applicant was being or in which he might expect to be educated or trained, and where the application is made by virtue of section 1(1)(d) the court shall also have regard–

(a)   to whether the deceased had assumed any responsibility for the applicant's maintenance and, if so, to the extent to which and the basis upon which the deceased assumed that responsibility and to the length of time for which the deceased discharged that responsibility;

(b)   to whether in assuming and discharging that responsibility the deceased did so knowing that the applicant was not his own child;

(c)   to the liability of any other person to maintain the applicant.

(4)   Without prejudice to the generality of paragraph (g) of subsection (1) above, where an application for an order under section 2 of this Act is made by virtue of section 1(1)(e) of this Act, the court shall, in addition to the matters specifically mentioned in paragraphs (a) to (f) of that subsection, have regard to the extent to which and the basis upon which the deceased assumed responsibility for the maintenance of the applicant, and to the length of time for which the deceased discharged that responsibility.

(5)   In considering the matters to which the court is required to have regard under this section, the court shall take into account the facts as known to the court at the date of the hearing.

(6)   In considering the financial resources of any person for the purposes of this section the court shall take into account his earning capacity and in considering the financial needs

of any person for the purposes of this section the court shall take into account his financial obligations and responsibilities.

4 Time-limit for applications

An application for an order under section 2 of this Act shall not, except with the permission of the court, be made after the end of the period of six months from the date on which representation with respect to the estate of the deceased is first taken out.

5 Interim orders

(1) Where an application for an order under section 3 of this Act it appears to the court–

    (a) that the applicant is in immediate need of financial assistance, but it is not yet possible to determine what order (if any) should be made under that section; and

    (b) that property forming part of the net estate of the deceased is or can be made available to meet the need of the applicant;

the court may order that, subject to such conditions or restrictions, if any, as the court may impose and to any further order of the court, there shall be paid to the applicant out of the net estate of the deceased such sum or sums and (if more than one) at such intervals as the court thinks reasonable; and the court may order that, subject to the provisions of this Act, such payments are to be made until such date as the court may specify, not being later than the date on which the court either makes an order under the said section 2 or decides not to exercise its powers under that section.

(2) Subsections (2), (3) and (4) of section 2 of this Act shall apply in relation to an order under this section as they apply in relation to an order under that section.

(3) In determining what order, if any, should be made under this section the court shall, so far as the urgency of the case admits, have regard to the same matters as those to which the court is required to have regard under section 3 of this Act.

(4) An order made under section 2 of this Act may provide that any sum paid to the applicant by virtue of this section shall be treated to such an extent and in such manner as may be provided by that order as having been paid on account of any payment provided for by that order.

6 Variation, discharge, etc of orders for periodical payments

(1) Subject to the provisions of this Act, where the court has made an order under section 2(1)(a) of this Act (in this section referred to as 'the original order') for the making of periodical payments to any person (in this section referred to as 'the original recipient'), the court, on an application under this section, shall have power by order to vary or discharge the original order or to suspend any provision of it temporarily and to revive the operation of any provision so suspended.

(2) Without prejudice to the generality of subsection (1) above, an order made on an application for the variation of the original order may–

    (a) provide for the making out of any relevant property of such periodical payments and for such term as may be specified in the order to any person who has applied, or would but for section 4 of this Act be entitled to apply, for an order under section 2 of this Act (whether or not, in the case of any application, an order was made in favour of the applicant);

    (b) provide for the payment out of any relevant property of a lump sum of such amount as may be so specified to the original recipient or to any such person as is mentioned in paragraph (a) above;

(c)   provide for the transfer of the relevant property, or such part thereof as may be so specified, to the original recipient or to any such person as is so mentioned.

(3)   Where the original order provides that any periodical payments payable thereunder to the original recipient are to cease on the occurrence of an event specified in the order (other than the formation of a subsequent marriage or civil partnership by a former spouse or former civil partner) or on the expiration of a period so specified, then, if, before the end of the period of six months from the date of the occurrence of that event or of the expiration of that period, an application is made for an order under this section, the court shall have power to make any order which it would have had power to make if the application had been made before the date (whether in favour of the original recipient or any such person as is mentioned in subsection (2)(a) above and whether having effect from that date or from such later date as the court may specify).

(4)   Any reference in this section to the original order shall include a reference to an order made under this section and any reference in this section to the original recipient shall include a reference to any person to whom periodical payments are required to be made by virtue of an order under this section.

(5)   An application under this section may be made by any of the following persons, that is to say–

(a)   any person who by virtue of section 1(1) of this Act has applied, or would but for section 4 of this Act be entitled to apply, for an order under section 2 of this Act,

(b)   the personal representatives of the deceased,

(c)   the trustees of any relevant property, and

(d)   any beneficiary of the estate of the deceased.

(6)   An order under this section may only affect–

(a)   property the income of which is at the date of the order applicable wholly or in part for the making of periodical payments to any person who has applied for an order under this Act, or

(b)   in the case of an application under subsection (3) above in respect of payments which have ceased to be payable on the occurrence of an event or the expiration of a period, property the income of which was so applicable immediately before the occurrence of that event or the expiration of that period, as the case may be,

and any such property as is mentioned in paragraph (a) or (b) above is in subsections (2) and (5) above referred to as 'relevant property'.

(7)   In exercising the powers conferred by this section the court shall have regard to all circumstances of the case, including any change in any of the matters to which the court was required to have regard when making the order to which the application relates.

(8)   Where the court makes an order under this section, it may give such consequential directions as it thinks necessary or expedient having regard to the provisions of the order.

(9)   No such order as is mentioned in section 2(1)(d), (e) or (f), 9, 10 or 11 of this Act shall be made on an application under this section.

(10)   For the avoidance of doubt it is hereby declared that, in relation to an order which provides for the making of periodical payments which are to cease on the occurrence of an event specified in the order (other than the formation of a subsequent marriage or civil partnership by a former spouse or former civil partner) or on the expiration of a period so specified, the power to vary an order includes power to provide for the making of periodical payments after the expiration of that period or the occurrence of that event.

7 Payment of lump sums by instalments

(1)   An order under section 2(1)(b) or 6(2)(b) of this Act for the payment of a lump sum may provide for the payment of that sum by instalments of such amount as may be specified in the order.

(2)   Where an order is made by virtue of subsection (1) above, the court shall have power, on an application made by the person to whom the lump sum is payable, by the personal representatives of the deceased or by the trustees of the property out of which the lump sum is payable, to vary that order by varying the number of instalments payable, the amount of any instalment and the date on which any instalment becomes payable.

Property available for financial provision

8 Property treated as part of 'net estate'

(1)   Where a deceased person has in accordance with the provisions of any enactment nominated any person to receive any sum of money or other property on his death and that nomination is in force at the time of his death, that sum of money, after deducting therefrom any inheritance tax payable in respect thereof, or that other property, to the extent of the value thereof at the date of the death of the deceased after deducting therefrom any inheritance tax so payable, shall be treated for the purposes of this Act as part of the net estate of the deceased; but this subsection shall not render any person liable for having paid that sum or transferred that other property to the person named in the nomination in accordance with the directions given in the nomination.

(2)   Where any sum of money or other property is received by any person as a donatio mortis causa made by a deceased person, that sum of money, after deducting therefrom any inheritance tax payable thereon, or that other property, to the extent of the value thereof at the date of the death of the deceased after deducting therefrom any inheritance tax so payable, shall be treated for the purposes of this Act as part of the net estate of the deceased; but this subsection shall not render any person liable for having paid that sum or transferred that other property in order to give effect to that donatio mortis causa.

(3)   The amount of inheritance tax to be deducted for the purposes of this section shall not exceed the amount of that tax which has been borne by the person nominated by the deceased or, as the case may be, the person who has received a sum of money or other property as a donatio mortis causa.

9 Property held on a joint tenancy

(1)   Where a deceased person was immediately before his death beneficially entitled to a joint tenancy of any property, then, if, before the end of the period of six months from the date on which representation with respect to the estate of the deceased was first taken out, an application is made for an order under section 2 of this Act, the court for the purpose of facilitating the making of financial provision for the applicant under this Act may order that the deceased's severable share of that property, at the value thereof immediately before his death, shall, to such extent as appears to the court to be just in all the circumstances of the case, be treated for the purposes of this Act as part of the net estate of the deceased.

(2)   In determining the extent to which any severable share is to be treated as part of the net estate of the deceased by virtue of an order under subsection (1) above, the court shall have regard to any inheritance tax payable in respect of that severable share.

(3)   Where an order is made under subsection (1) above, the provisions of this section shall not render any person liable for anything done by him before the order was made.

(4)   For the avoidance of doubt it is hereby declared that for the purposes of this section there may be a joint tenancy of a chose in action.

Powers of court in relation to transactions intended to defeat applications for financial provision

10   Dispositions intended to defeat applications for financial provision

(1)   Where an application is made to the court for an order under section 2 of this Act, the applicant may, in the proceedings on that application, apply to the court for an order under subsection (2) below.

(2)   Where on an application under subsection (1) above the court is satisfied—

   (a)   that, less than six years before the date of the death of the deceased, the deceased with the intention of defeating an application for financial provision under this Act made a disposition, and

   (b)   that full valuable consideration for that disposition was not given by the person to whom or for the benefit of whom the disposition was made (in this section referred to as 'the donee') or by any other person, and

   (c)   that the exercise of the powers conferred by this section would facilitate the making of financial provision for the applicant under this Act,

then, subject to the provisions of this section and of sections 12 and 13 of this Act, the court may order the donee (whether or not at the date of the order he holds any interest in the property disposed of to him or for his benefit by the deceased) to provide, for the purpose of the making of that financial provision, such sum of money or other property as may be specified in the order.

(3)   Where an order is made under subsection (2) above as respects any disposition made by the deceased which consisted of the payment of money to or for the benefit of the donee, the amount of any sum of money or the value of any property ordered to be provided under that subsection shall not exceed the amount of the payment made by the deceased after deducting therefrom any inheritance tax borne by the donee in respect of that payment.

(4)   Where an order is made under subsection (2) above as respects any disposition made by the deceased which consisted of the transfer of property (other than a sum of money) to or for the benefit of the donee, the amount of any sum of money or the value of any property ordered to be provided under that subsection shall not exceed the value at the date of the death of the deceased of the property disposed of by him to or for the benefit of the donee (or if that property has been disposed of by the person to whom it was transferred by the deceased, the value at the date of that disposal thereof) after deducting therefrom any inheritance tax borne by the donee in respect of the transfer of that property by the deceased.

(5)   Where an application (in this subsection referred to as 'the original application') is made for an order under subsection (2) above in relation to any disposition, then, if on an application under this subsection by the donee or by any applicant for an order under section 2 of this Act the court is satisfied—

   (a)   that, less than six years before the date of the death of the deceased, the deceased with the intention of defeating an application for financial provision under this Act made a disposition other than the disposition which is the subject of the original application, and

   (b)   that full valuable consideration for that other disposition was not given by the person to whom or for the benefit of whom that other disposition was made or by any other person, the court may exercise in relation to the person to whom or for the benefit of whom that other disposition was made the powers which the court would have had under subsection (2) above if the original application had been made in respect of that other disposition and the court had been satisfied as to the matters set out in paragraphs (a), (b) and (c) of that subsection; and where any application is made under this subsection, any reference in this section (except in subsection (2)(b)) to the donee shall include a reference to the person to whom or for the benefit of whom that other disposition was made.

(6)   In determining whether and in what manner to exercise its powers under this section, the court shall have regard to the circumstances in which any disposition was made and any valuable consideration which was given therefor, the relationship, if any, of the donee to the deceased, the conduct and financial resources of the donee and all the other circumstances of the case.

(7)   In this section 'disposition' does not include–

(a)   any provision in a will, any such nomination as is mentioned in section 8(1) of this Act or any donatio mortis causa, or

(b)   any appointment of property made, otherwise than by will, in the exercise of a special power of appointment,

but, subject to these exceptions, includes any payment of money (including the payment of a premium under a policy of assurance) and any conveyance, assurance, appointment or gift of property of any description, whether made by an instrument or otherwise.

(8)   The provisions of this section do not apply to any disposition made before the commencement of this Act.

11   Contracts to leave property by will

(1)   Where an application is made to a court for an order under section 2 of this Act, the applicant may, in the proceedings on that application, apply to the court for an order under this section.

(2)   Where on an application under subsection (1) above the court is satisfied–

(a)   that the deceased made a contract by which he agreed to leave by his will a sum of money or other property to any person or by which he agreed that a sum of money or other property would be paid or transferred to any person out of his estate, and

(b)   that the deceased made that contract with the intention of defeating an application for financial provision under this Act, and

(c)   that when the contract was made full valuable consideration for that contract was not given or promised by the person with whom or for the benefit of whom the contract was made (in this section referred to as 'the donee') or by any other person, and

(d)   that the exercise of the powers conferred by this section would facilitate the making of financial provision for the applicant under this Act,

then, subject to the provisions of this section and of sections 12 and 13 of this Act, the court may make any one or more of the following orders, that is to say–

(i)   if any money has been paid or any other property has been transferred to or for the benefit of the donee in accordance with the contract, an order directing the donee to provide, for the purpose of the making of that financial provision, such sum of money or other property as may be specified in the order;

(ii)   if the money or all the money has not been paid or the property or all the property has not been transferred in accordance with the contract, an order directing the personal representatives not to make any payment or transfer any property, or not to make any further payment or transfer any further property, as the case may be, in accordance therewith or directing the personal representatives only to make such payment or transfer such property as may be specified in the order.

(3) Notwithstanding anything in subsection (2) above, the court may exercise its powers thereunder in relation to any contract made by the deceased only to the extent that the court considers that the amount of any sum of money paid or to be paid or the value of any property transferred or to be transferred in accordance with the contract exceeds the value of any valuable consideration given or to be given for that contract, and for this purpose the court shall have regard to the value of property at the date of the hearing.

(4) In determining whether and in what manner to exercise its powers under this section, the court shall have regard to the circumstances in which the contract was made, the relationship, if any, of the donee to the deceased, the conduct and financial resources of the donee and all the other circumstances of the case.

(5) Where an order has been made under subsection (2) above in relation to any contract the rights of any person to enforce that contract or to recover damages or to obtain other relief for the breach thereof shall be subject to any adjustment made by the court under section 12(3) of this Act and shall survive to such extent only as is consistent with giving effect to the terms of that order.

(6) The provisions of this section do not apply to a contract made before the commencement of this Act.

12 Provisions supplementary to ss 10 and 11

(1) Where the exercise of any of the powers conferred by section 10 or 11 of this Act is conditional on the court being satisfied that a disposition or contract was made by a deceased person with the intention of defeating an application for financial provision under this Act, that condition shall be fulfilled if the court is of the opinion that, on a balance of probabilities, the intention of the deceased (though not necessarily his sole intention) in making the disposition or contract was to prevent an order for financial provision being made under this Act or to reduce the amount of the provision which might otherwise be granted by an order thereunder.

(2) Where an application is made under section 11 of this Act with respect to any contract made by the deceased and no valuable consideration was given or promised by any person for that contract then, notwithstanding anything in subsection (1) above, it shall be presumed, unless the contrary is shown, that the deceased made that contract with the intention of defeating an application for financial provision under this Act.

(3) Where the court makes an order under section 10 or 11 of this Act it may give such consequential directions as it thinks fit (including directions requiring the making of any payment or the transfer of any property) for giving effect to the order or for securing a fair adjustment of the rights of the persons affected thereby.

(4) Any power conferred on the court by the said section 10 or 11 to order the donee, in relation to any disposition or contract, to provide any sum of money or other property shall be exercisable in like manner in relation to the personal representative of the donee, and–

(a) any reference in section 10(4) to the disposal of property by the donee shall include a reference to disposal by the personal representative of the donee, and

(b) any reference in section 10(5) to an application by the donee under that subsection shall include a reference to an application by the personal representative of the donee;

but the court shall not have power under the said section 10 or 11 to make an order in respect of any property forming part of the estate of the donee which has been distributed by the personal representative; and the personal representative shall not be liable for having distributed any such property before he has notice of the making of an application under the said section 10 or 11 on the ground that he ought to have taken into account the possibility that such an application would be made.

13 Provisions as to trustees in relation to ss 10 and 11

(1)   Where an application is made for–

(a)   an order under section 10 of this Act in respect of a disposition made by the deceased to any person as a trustee, or

(b)   an order under section 11 of this Act in respect of any payment made or property transferred, in accordance with a contract made by the deceased, to any person as a trustee,

the powers of the court under the said section 10 or 11 to order that trustee to provide a sum of money or other property shall be subject to the following limitation (in addition, in a case of an application under section 10, to any provision regarding the deduction of inheritance tax) namely, that the amount of any sum of money or the value of any property ordered to be provided–

(i)   in the case of an application in respect of a disposition which consisted of the payment of money or an application in respect of the payment of money in accordance with a contract, shall not exceed the aggregate of so much of that money as is at the date of the order in the hands of the trustee and the value at that date of any property which represents that money or is derived therefrom and is at that date in the hands of the trustee;

(ii)   in the case of an application in respect of a disposition which consisted of the transfer of property (other than a sum of money) or an application in respect of the transfer of property (other than a sum of money) in accordance with a contract, shall not exceed the aggregate of the value at the date of the order of so much of that property as is at that date in the hands of the trustee and the value at that date of any property which represents the first mentioned property or is derived therefrom and is at that date in the hands of the trustee.

(2)   Where any such application is made in respect of a disposition made to any person as a trustee or in respect of any payment made or property transferred in pursuance of a contract to any person as a trustee, the trustee shall not be liable for having distributed any money or other property on the ground that he ought to have taken into account the possibility that such an application would be made.

(3)   Where any such application is made in respect of a disposition made to any person as a trustee or in respect of any payment made or property transferred in accordance with a contract to any person as a trustee, any reference in the said section 10 or 11 to the donee shall be construed as including a reference to the trustee or trustees for the time being of the trust in question and any reference in subsection (1) or (2) above to a trustee shall be construed in the same way.

Special provisions relating to cases of divorce, separation, etc

14 Provision as to cases where no financial relief was granted in divorce proceedings, etc

(1)   Where, within twelve months from the date on which a divorce order or separation order

has been made under the Family Law Act 1996 in relation to a marriage or a decree of nullity of marriage has been made absolute, a party to the marriage dies and–

(a) an application for a financial provision order under section 22A or 23 of the Matrimonial Causes Act 1973 or a property adjustment order under section 23A or 24 of that Act has not been made by the other party to that marriage, or

(b) such an application has been made but the proceedings thereon have not been determined at the time of the death of the deceased,

then, if an application for an order under section 2 of this Act is made by that other party, the court shall, notwithstanding anything in section 1 or section 3 of this Act, have power, if it thinks it just to do so, to treat that party for the purposes of that application as if, as the case may be, the divorce order or separation order had not been made or the decree of nullity had not been made absolute.

(2) This section shall not apply in relation to a separation order unless at the date of the death of the deceased the order was in force and the separation was continuing.

14A Provision as to cases where no financial relief was granted in proceedings for the dissolution etc of a civil partnership

(1) Subsection (2) below applies where–

(a) a dissolution order, nullity order, separation order or presumption of death order has been made under Chapter 2 of Part 2 of the Civil Partnership Act 2004 in relation to a civil partnership,

(b) one of the civil partners dies within twelve months from the date on which the order is made, and

(c) either–

(i) an application for a financial provision order under Part 1 of Schedule 5 to that Act or a property adjustment order under Part 2 of that Schedule has not been made by the other civil partner, or

(ii) such an application has been made but the proceedings on the application have not been determined at the time of the death of the deceased.

(2) If an application for an order under section 2 of this Act is made by the surviving civil partner, the court shall, notwithstanding anything in section 1 or section 3 of this Act, have power, if it thinks it just to do so, to treat the surviving civil partner as if the order mentioned in subsection (1)(a) above had not been made.

(3) This section shall not apply in relation to a separation order unless at the date of the death of the deceased the separation order was in force and the separation was continuing.

15 Restriction imposed in divorce proceedings, etc on application under this Act

(1) At any time when the court–

(a) has jurisdiction under section 23A or 24 of the Matrimonial Causes Act 1973 to make a property adjustment order in relation to a marriage; or

(b) would have such jurisdiction if either the jurisdiction had not already been exercised or an application for such an order were made with the leave of the court,

the court, if it considers it just to do so, may, on the application of either party to the marriage, order that the other party to the marriage shall not on the death of the applicant be entitled to apply for an order under section 2 of this Act.

In this subsection 'the court' means the High Court or, where a county court has jurisdiction by virtue of Part V of the Matrimonial and Family Proceedings Act 1984, a county court.

(2)   An order made under subsection (1) above with respect to any party to a marriage has effect in accordance with subsection (3) below at any time–

    (a)   after the marriage has been dissolved;

    (b)   after a decree of nullity has been made absolute in relation to the marriage; and

    (c)   while a separation order under the Family Law Act 1996 is in force in relation to the marriage and the separation is continuing.

(3)   If at any time when an order made under subsection (1) above with respect to any party to a marriage has effect the other party to the marriage dies, the court shall not entertain any application made by the surviving party to the marriage for an order under section 2 of this Act.

15ZA   Restriction imposed in proceedings for the dissolution etc of a civil partnership on application under this Act

(1)   On making a dissolution order, nullity order, separation order or presumption of death order under Chapter 2 of Part 2 of the Civil Partnership Act 2004, or at any time after making such an order, the court, if it considers it just to do so, may, on the application of either of the civil partners, order that the other civil partner shall not on the death of the applicant be entitled to apply for an order under section 2 of this Act.

(2)   In subsection (1) above 'the court' means the High Court or, where a county court has jurisdiction by virtue of Part 5 of the Matrimonial and Family Proceedings Act 1984, a county court.

(3)   In the case of a dissolution order, nullity order or presumption of death order ('the main order') an order may be made under subsection (1) above before (as well as after) the main order is made final, but if made before the main order is made final it shall not take effect unless the main order is made final.

(4)   Where an order under subsection (1) above made in connection with a dissolution order, nullity order or presumption of death order has come into force with respect to a civil partner, then, on the death of the other civil partner, the court shall not entertain any application for an order under section 2 of this Act made by the surviving civil partner.

(5)   Where an order under subsection (1) above made in connection with a separation order has come into force with respect to a civil partner, then, if the other civil partner dies while the separation order is in force and the separation is continuing, the court shall not entertain any application for an order under section 2 of this Act made by the surviving civil partner.

15A   Restriction imposed in proceedings under Matrimonial and Family Proceedings Act 1984 on application under this Act

(1)   On making an order under section 17 of the Matrimonial and Family Proceedings Act 1984 (orders for financial provision and property adjustment following overseas divorces, etc) the court, if it considers it just to do so, may, on the application of either party to the marriage, order that the other party to the marriage shall not on the death of the applicant be entitled to apply for an order under section 2 of this Act.

In this subsection 'the court' means the High Court or, where a county court has jurisdiction by virtue of Part V of the Matrimonial and Family Proceedings Act 1984, a county court.

(2)   Where an order under subsection (1) above has been made with respect to a party to a

marriage which has been dissolved or annulled, then, on the death of the other party to that marriage, the court shall not entertain an application under section 2 of this Act made by the first-mentioned party.

(3)   Where an order under subsection (1) above has been made with respect to a party to a marriage the parties to which have been legally separated, then, if the other party to the marriage dies while the legal separation is in force, the court shall not entertain an application under section 2 of this Act made by the first-mentioned party.

15B   Restriction imposed in proceedings under Schedule 7 to the Civil Partnership Act 2004 on application under this Act

(1)   On making an order under paragraph 9 of Schedule 7 to the Civil Partnership Act 2004 (orders for financial provision, property adjustment and pension-sharing following overseas dissolution etc of civil partnership) the court, if it considers it just to do so, may, on the application of either of the civil partners, order that the other civil partner shall not on the death of the applicant be entitled to apply for an order under section 2 of this Act.

(2)   In subsection (1) above 'the court' means the High Court or, where a county court has jurisdiction by virtue of Part 5 of the Matrimonial and Family Proceedings Act 1984, a county court.

(3)   Where an order under subsection (1) above has been made with respect to one of the civil partners in a case where a civil partnership has been dissolved or annulled, then, on the death of the other civil partner, the court shall not entertain an application under section 2 of this Act made by the surviving civil partner.

(4)   Where an order under subsection (1) above has been made with respect to one of the civil partners in a case where civil partners have been legally separated, then, if the other civil partner dies while the legal separation is in force, the court shall not entertain an application under section 2 of this Act made by the surviving civil partner.

16   Variation and discharge of secured periodical payments orders made under Matrimonial Causes Act 1973

(1)   Where an application for an order under section 2 of this Act is made to the court by any person who was at the time of the death of the deceased entitled to payments from the deceased under a secured periodical payments order made under the Matrimonial Causes Act 1973 or Schedule 5 to the Civil Partnership Act 2004, then, in the proceedings on that application, the court shall have power, if an application is made under this section by that person or by the personal representative of the deceased, to vary or discharge that periodical payments order or to revive the operation of any provision thereof which has been suspended under section 31 of that Act of 1973 or Part 11 of that Schedule.

(2)   In exercising the powers conferred by this section the court shall have regard to all the circumstances of the case, including any order which the court proposes to make under section 2 or section 5 of this Act and any change (whether resulting from the death of the deceased or otherwise) in any of the matters to which the court was required to have regard when making the secured periodical payments order.

(3)   The powers exercisable by the court under this section in relation to an order shall be exercisable also in relation to any instrument executed in pursuance of the order.

17   Variation and revocation of maintenance agreements

(1)   Where an application for an order under section 2 of this Act is made to the court by any person who was at the time of the death of the deceased entitled to payments from the

deceased under a maintenance agreement which provided for the continuation of payments under the agreement after the death of the deceased, then, in the proceedings on that application, the court shall have power, if an application is made under this section by that person or by the personal representative of the deceased, to vary or revoke that agreement.

(2)   In exercising the powers conferred by this section the court shall have regard to all the circumstances of the case, including any order which the court proposes to make under section 2 or section 5 of this Act and any change (whether resulting from the death of the deceased or otherwise) in any of the circumstances in the light of which the agreement was made.

(3)   If a maintenance agreement is varied by the court under this section the like consequences shall ensue as if the variation had been made immediately before the death of the deceased by agreement between the parties and for valuable consideration.

(4)   In this section 'maintenance agreement', in relation to a deceased person, means any agreement made, whether in writing or not and whether before or after the commencement of this Act, by the deceased with any person with whom he formed a marriage or civil partnership, being an agreement which contained provisions governing the rights and liabilities towards one another when living separately of the parties to that marriage or of the civil partners (whether or not the marriage or civil partnership has been dissolved or annulled) in respect of the making or securing of payments or the disposition or use of any property, including such rights and liabilities with respect to the maintenance or education of any child, whether or not a child of the deceased or a person who was treated by the deceased as a child of the family in relation to that marriage or civil partnership.

18   Availability of court's powers under this Act in applications under ss 31 and 36 of the Matrimonial Causes Act 1973

(1)   Where–

    (a)   a person against whom a secured periodical payments order was made under the Matrimonial Causes Act 1973 has died and an application is made under section 31(6) of that Act for the variation or discharge of that order or for the revival of the operation of any provision thereof which has been suspended, or

    (b)   a party to a maintenance agreement within the meaning of section 34 of that Act has died, the agreement being one which provides for the continuation of payments thereunder after the death of one of the parties, and an application is made under section 36(1) of that Act for the alteration of the agreement under section 35 thereof,

the court shall have power to direct that the application made under the said section 31(6) or 36(1) shall be deemed to have been accompanied by an application for an order under section 2 of this Act.

(2)   Where the court gives a direction under subsection (1) above it shall have power, in the proceedings on the application under the said section 31(6) or 36(1), to make any order which the court would have had power to make under the provisions of this Act if the application under the said section 31(6) or 36(1), as the case may be, had been made jointly with an application for an order under the said section 2; and the court shall have power to give such consequential directions as may be necessary for enabling the court to exercise any of the powers available to the court under this Act in the case of an application for an order under section 2.

(3)   Where an order made under section 15(1) of this Act is in force with respect to a party to

a marriage, the court shall not give a direction under subsection (1) above with respect to any application made under the said section 31(6) or 36(1) by that party on the death of the other party.

18A   Availability of court's powers under this Act in applications under paragraphs 60 and 73 of Schedule 5 to the Civil Partnership Act 2004

(1)   Where–

(a)   a person against whom a secured periodical payments order was made under Schedule 5 to the Civil Partnership Act 2004 has died and an application is made under paragraph 60 of that Schedule for the variation or discharge of that order or for the revival of the operation of any suspended provision of the order, or

(b)   a party to a maintenance agreement within the meaning of Part 13 of that Schedule has died, the agreement being one which provides for the continuation of payments under the agreement after the death of one of the parties, and an application is made under paragraph 73 of that Schedule for the alteration of the agreement under paragraph 69 of that Schedule,

the court shall have power to direct that the application made under paragraph 60 or 73 of that Schedule shall be deemed to have been accompanied by an application for an order under section 2 of this Act.

(2)   Where the court gives a direction under subsection (1) above it shall have power, in the proceedings on the application under paragraph 60 or 73 of that Schedule, to make any order which the court would have had power to make under the provisions of this Act if the application under that paragraph had been made jointly with an application for an order under section 2 of this Act; and the court shall have power to give such consequential directions as may be necessary for enabling the court to exercise any of the powers available to the court under this Act in the case of an application for an order under section 2.

(3)   Where an order made under section 15ZA(1) of this Act is in force with respect to a civil partner, the court shall not give a direction under subsection (1) above with respect to any application made under paragraph 60 or 73 of that Schedule by that civil partner on the death of the other civil partner.

Miscellaneous and supplementary provisions

19   Effect, duration and form of orders

(1)   Where an order is made under section 2 of this Act then for all purposes, including the purposes of the enactments relating to inheritance tax, the will or the law relating to intestacy, or both the will and the law relating to intestacy, as the case may be, shall have effect and be deemed to have had effect as from the deceased's death subject to the provisions of the order.

(2)   Any order made under section 2 or 5 of this Act in favour of–

(a)   an applicant who was the former spouse or former civil partner of the deceased, or

(b)   an applicant who was the husband or wife of the deceased in a case where, at the date of death, a separation order under the Family Law Act 1996 was in force in relation to the marriage with the deceased and the separation was continuing, or

(c)   an applicant who was the civil partner of the deceased in a case where, at the date of death, a separation order under Chapter 2 of Part 2 of the Civil Partnership Act 2004 was in force in relation to their civil partnership and the separation was continuing, shall, in so far as it provides for the making of periodical payments, cease to have effect on the formation by the applicant of a subsequent marriage or civil partnership, except in relation to any arrears due under the order on the date of the formation of the subsequent marriage or civil partnership.

(3)   A copy of every order made under this Act other than an order made under section 15(1) or 15ZA(1) of this Act shall be sent to the principal registry of the Family Division for entry and filing, and a memorandum of the order shall be endorsed on, or permanently annexed to, the probate or letters of administration under which the estate is being administered.

20   Provisions as to personal representatives

(1)   The provisions of this Act shall not render the personal representative of a deceased person liable for having distributed any part of the estate of the deceased, after the end of the period of six months from the date on which representation with respect to the estate of the deceased is first taken out, on the ground that he ought to have taken into account the possibility–

(a)   that the court might permit the making of an application for an order under section 2 of this Act after the end of that period, or

(b)   that, where an order has been made under the said section 2, the court might exercise in relation thereto the powers conferred on it by section 6 of this Act,

but this subsection shall not prejudice any power to recover, by reason of the making of an order under this Act, any part of the estate so distributed.

(2)   Where the personal representative of a deceased person pays any sum directed by an order under section 5 of this Act to be paid out of the deceased's net estate, he shall not be under any liability by reason of that estate not being sufficient to make the payment, unless at the time of making the payment he has reasonable cause to believe that the estate is not sufficient.

(3)   Where a deceased person entered into a contract by which he agreed to leave by his will any sum of money or other property to any person or by which he agreed that a sum of money or other property would be paid or transferred to any person out of his estate, then, if the personal representative of the deceased has reason to believe that the deceased entered into the contract with the intention of defeating an application for financial provision under this Act, he may, notwithstanding anything in that contract, postpone the payment of that sum of money or the transfer of that property until the expiration of the period of six months from the date on which representation with respect to the estate of the deceased is first taken out or, if during that period an application is made for an order under section 2 of this Act, until the determination of the proceedings on that application.

21   [*repealed*]

22   [*repealed*]

23   Determination of date on which representation was first taken out

In considering for the purposes of this Act when representation with respect to the estate of a deceased person was first taken out, a grant limited to settled land or to trust property shall be left out of account, and a grant limited to real estate or to personal estate shall be left out of account unless a grant limited to the remainder of the estate has previously been made or is made at the same time.

24 Effect of this Act on s 46(1)(vi) of Administration of Estates Act 1925

Section 46(1)(vi) of the Administration of Estates Act 1925, in so far as it provides for the devolution of property on the Crown, the Duchy of Lancaster or the Duke of Cornwall as bona vacantia, shall have effect subject to the provisions of this Act.

25 Interpretation

(1) In this Act–

'beneficiary', in relation to the estate of a deceased person, means–

(a) a person who under the will of the deceased or under the law relating to intestacy is beneficially interested in the estate or would be so interested if an order had not been made under this Act, and

(b) a person who has received any sum of money or other property which by virtue of section 8(1) or 8(2) of this Act is treated as part of the net estate of the deceased or would have received that sum or other property if an order had not been made under this Act;

'child' includes an illegitimate child and a child en ventre sa mere at the death of the deceased;

'the court' unless the context otherwise requires means the High Court, or where a county court has jurisdiction by virtue of section 22 of this Act, a county court;

'former civil partner' means a person whose civil partnership with the deceased was during the lifetime of the deceased either–

(a) dissolved or annulled by an order made under the law of any part of the British Islands, or

(b) dissolved or annulled in any country or territory outside the British Islands by a dissolution or annulment which is entitled to be recognised as valid by the law of England and Wales;

'former spouse' means a person whose marriage with the deceased was during the lifetime of the deceased either–

(a) dissolved or annulled by an order or decree of divorce or a decree of nullity of marriage granted under the law of any part of the British Islands, or

(b) dissolved or annulled in any country or territory outside the British Islands by a divorce or annulment which is entitled to be recognised as valid by the law of England and Wales;

'net estate', in relation to a deceased person, means–

(a) all property of which the deceased had power to dispose by his will (otherwise than by virtue of a special power of appointment) less the amount of his funeral, testamentary and administration expenses, debts and liabilities, including any inheritance tax payable out of his estate on his death;

(b) any property in respect of which the deceased held a general power of appointment (not being a power exercisable by will) which has not been exercised;

(c) any sum of money or other property which is treated for the purposes of this Act as part of the net estate of the deceased by virtue of section 8(1) or (2) of this Act;

(d) any property which is treated for the purposes of this Act as part of the net estate of the deceased by virtue of an order made under section 9 of the Act;

(e) any sum of money or other property which is, by reason of a disposition or contract made by the deceased, ordered under section 10 or 11 of this Act to be provided for the purpose of the making of financial provision under this Act;

119

'property' includes any chose in action;

'reasonable financial provision' has the meaning assigned to it by section 1 of this Act;

'valuable consideration' does not include marriage or a promise of marriage;

'will' includes codicil.

(2)   For the purposes of paragraph (a) of the definition of 'net estate' in subsection (1) above a person who is not of full age and capacity shall be treated as having power to dispose by will of all property of which he would have had power to dispose by will if he had been of full age and capacity.

(3)   Any reference in this Act to provision out of the net estate of a deceased person includes a reference to provision extending to the whole of that estate.

(4)   For the purposes of this Act any reference to a spouse, wife or husband shall be treated as including a reference to a person who in good faith entered into a void marriage with the deceased unless either–

    (a)   the marriage of the deceased and that person was dissolved or annulled during the lifetime of the deceased and the dissolution or annulment is recognised by the law of England and Wales, or

    (b)   that person has during the lifetime of the deceased formed a subsequent marriage or civil partnership.

(4A)   For the purposes of this Act any reference to a civil partner shall be treated as including a reference to a person who in good faith formed a void civil partnership with the deceased unless either–

    (a)   the civil partnership between the deceased and that person was dissolved or annulled during the lifetime of the deceased and the dissolution or annulment is recognised by the law of England and Wales, or

    (b)   that person has during the lifetime of the deceased formed a subsequent civil partnership or marriage.

(5)   Any reference in this Act to the formation of, or to a person who has formed, a subsequent marriage or civil partnership includes (as the case may be) a reference to the formation of, or to a person who has formed, a marriage or civil partnership which is by law void or voidable.

(5A)   The formation of a marriage or civil partnership shall be treated for the purposes of this Act as the formation of a subsequent marriage or civil partnership, in relation to either of the spouses or civil partners, notwithstanding that the previous marriage or civil partnership of that spouse or civil partner was void or voidable.

(6)   Any reference in this Act to an order or decree made under the Matrimonial Causes Act 1973 or under any section of that Act shall be construed as including a reference to an order or decree which is deemed to have been made under that Act or under that section thereof, as the case may be.

(6A)   Any reference in this Act to an order made under, or under any provision of, the Civil Partnership Act 2004 shall be construed as including a reference to anything which is deemed to be an order made (as the case may be) under that Act or provision.

(7)   Any reference in this Act to any enactment is a reference to that enactment as amended by or under any subsequent enactment.

26   Consequential amendments, repeals and transitional provisions

(1)   [*repealed*]

(2)   Subject to the provisions of this section, the enactments specified in the Schedule to this Act are hereby repealed to the extent specified in the third column of the Schedule;

(3)   The repeal of the said enactment shall not affect their operation in relation to any application made thereunder (whether before or after the commencement of this Act) with reference to the death of any person who died before the commencement of this Act.

(4)   Without prejudice to the provisions of section 38 of the Interpretation Act 1889 (which relates to the effect of repeals) nothing in any repeal made by this Act shall affect any order made or direction given under any enactment repealed by this Act, and, subject to the provisions of this Act, every such order or direction (other than an order made under section 4A of the Inheritance (Family Provision) Act 1938 or section 28A of the Matrimonial Causes Act 1965) shall, if it is in force at the commencement of this Act or is made by virtue of subsection (2) above, continue in force as if it had been made under section 2(1)(a) of this Act, and for the purposes of section 6(7) of this Act the court in exercising its powers under that section in relation to an order continued in force by this subsection shall be required to have regard to any change in any of the circumstances to which the court would have been required to have regard when making that order if the order had been made with reference to the death of any person who died after the commencement of this Act.

27   Short title, commencement and extent

(1)   This Act may be cited as the Inheritance (Provision for Family and Dependants) Act 1975.

(2)   This Act does not extend to Scotland or Northern Ireland.

(3)   This Act shall come into force on 1st April 1976.

SCHEDULE – ENACTMENTS REPEALED

Section 26

Chapter	Short Title	Extent of Repeal
1938 c 72	The Inheritance (Family Provision) Act 1938	The whole Act.
1952 c 64	The Intestates' Estates Act 1952	Section 7 and Schedule 3.
1965 c 72	The Matrimonial Causes Act 1965	Section 26 to 28(A) and section 25(4) and (5) as applied by section 28(2).
1966 c 35	The Family Provision Act 1966	The whole Act, except section 1 and subsections (1) and (3) of section 10.
1969 c 46	The Family Law Reform Act 1969	Sections 5(1) and 18.
1970 c 31	The Administration of Justice Act 1970	In Schedule 2, paragraph 16.

1970 c 33	The Law Reform (Miscellaneous Provisions) Act 1970	Section 6.
1970 c 45	The Matrimonial Proceedings and Property Act 1970	Section 36.
1971 c 23	The Courts Act 1971	Section 45(1)(a).
1973 c 18	The Matrimonial Causes Act 1973	In section 50, in subsection (1)(a) the words from 'and sections 26' to the end of the paragraph, in subsection (1)(d) the words 'or sections 26 to 28A of the Matrimonial Causes Act 1965' and in subsection (2)(a) the words 'or under section 26 or 27 of the Matrimonial Causes Act 1965'. In Schedule 2, paragraph 5(1) and in paragraph 12 the words '(a) sections 26 to 28A of the Matrimonial Causes Act 1965'.
1975 c 7	The Finance Act 1975	In Schedule 12, paragraph 6.

Intestates' Estates Act 1952, s.5 and Sched.2

PART 1 – AMENDMENTS OF LAW OF INTESTATE SUCCESSION

5 Rights of surviving spouse or civil partner as respects the matrimonial or civil partnership home

The Second Schedule to this Act shall have effect for enabling the surviving spouse or civil partner of a person dying intestate after the commencement of this Act to acquire the matrimonial or civil partnership home.

SCHEDULE 2 – RIGHTS OF SURVIVING SPOUSE OR CIVIL PARTNER AS RESPECTS THE MATRIMONIAL OR CIVIL PARTNERSHIP HOME

1   (1)   Subject to the provisions of this Schedule, where the residuary estate of the intestate comprises of interest in a dwelling-house in which the surviving spouse or civil partner was resident at the time of the intestate's death, the surviving spouse or civil partner may require the personal representative in exercise of the power conferred by section forty-one of the principal Act (and with due regard to the requirements of that section as to valuation) to appropriate the said interest in the dwelling-house in or towards satisfaction of any absolute interest of the surviving spouse or civil partner in the real and personal estate of the intestate.

    (2)   The right conferred by this paragraph shall not be exercisable where the interest is–

        (a)   a tenancy which at the date of the death of the intestate was a tenancy which would determine within the period of two years from that date; or

        (b)   a tenancy which the landlord by notice given for that date could determine within the remainder of that period.

    (3)   Nothing in subsection (5) of section forty-one of the principal Act (which requires the personal representative, in making an appropriation to any person under that section, to have regard to the rights of others) shall prevent the personal representative from giving effect to the right conferred by this paragraph.

    (4)   The reference in this paragraph to an absolute interest in the real and personal estate of the intestate includes a reference to the capital value of a life interest which the surviving spouse or civil partner has under this Act elected to have redeemed.

    (5)   Where part of a building was, at the date of the death of the intestate, occupied as a separate dwelling, that dwelling shall for the purposes of this Schedule be treated as a dwelling-house.

2   Where–

        (a)   the dwelling-house forms part of a building and an interest in the whole of the building is comprised in the residuary estate; or

(b)   the dwelling-house is held with agricultural land and an interest in the agricultural land is comprised in the residuary estate; or

(c)   the whole or part of the dwelling-house was at the time of the intestate's death used as a hotel or lodging house; or

(d)   a part of the dwelling-house was at the time of the intestate's death used for purposes other than domestic purposes,

the right conferred by paragraph 1 of this Schedule shall not be exercisable unless the court, on being satisfied that the exercise of that right is not likely to diminish the value of assets in the residuary estate (other than the said interest in the dwelling-house) or make them more difficult to dispose of, so orders.

3   (1)   The right conferred by paragraph 1 of this Schedule.

(a)   shall not be exercisable after the expiration of twelve months from the first taking out of representation with respect to the intestate's estate;

(b)   shall not be exercisable after the death of the surviving spouse or civil partner;

(c)   shall be exercisable, except where the surviving spouse or civil partner is the sole personal representative, by notifying the personal representative (or, where there are two or more personal representatives of whom one is the surviving spouse or civil partner, all of them except the surviving spouse or civil partner) in writing.

(2)   A notification in writing under paragraph (c) of the foregoing sub-paragraph shall not be revocable except with the consent of the personal representative; but the surviving spouse or civil partner may require the personal representative to have the said interest in the dwelling-house valued in accordance with section forty-one of the principal Act and to inform him or her of the result of that valuation before he or she decides whether to exercise the right.

(3)   Subsection (9) of the section forty-seven A added to the principal Act by section two of this Act shall apply for the purposes of the construction of the reference in this paragraph to the first taking out of representation, and the promise to subsection (5) of that section shall apply for the purpose of enabling the surviving spouse or civil partner to apply for an extension of the period of twelve months mentioned in this paragraph.

4   (1)   During the period of twelve months mentioned in paragraph 3 of this Schedule the personal representative shall not without the written consent of the surviving spouse or civil partner sell or otherwise dispose of the said interest in the dwelling-house except in the course of administration owing to want of other assets.

(2)   An application to the court under paragraph 2 of this Schedule may be made by the personal representative as well as by the surviving spouse or civil partner, and if, on an application under that paragraph, the court does not order that the right conferred by paragraph 1 of this Schedule shall be exercisable by the surviving spouse or civil partner, the court may authorise the personal representative to dispose of the said interest in the dwelling-house within the said period of twelve months.

(3)   Where the court under sub-paragraph (3) of paragraph 3 of this Schedule extends the said period of twelve months, the court may direct that this paragraph shall apply in relation to the extended period as it applied in relation to the original period of twelve months.

(4)   This paragraph shall not apply where the surviving spouse or civil partner is the sole personal representative or one of two or more personal representatives.

(5) Nothing in this paragraph shall confer any right on the surviving spouse or civil partner as against a purchaser from the personal representative.

5 (1) Where the surviving spouse or civil partner is one of two or more personal representatives, the rule that a trustee may not be a purchaser of trust property shall not prevent the surviving spouse or civil partner from purchasing out of the estate of the intestate an interest in a dwelling-house in which the surviving spouse or civil partner was resident at the time of the intestate's death.

(2) The power of appropriation under section forty-one of the principal Act shall include power to appropriate an interest in a dwelling-house in which the surviving spouse or civil partner was resident at the time of the intestate's death partly in satisfaction of an interest of the surviving spouse or civil partner in the real and personal estate of the intestate and partly in return for a payment of money by the surviving spouse or civil partner to the personal representative.

6 (1) Where the surviving spouse or civil partner lacks capacity (within the meaning of the Mental Capacity Act 2005) to make a requirement or give a consent under this Schedule, the requirement or consent may be made or given by a deputy appointed by the Court of Protection with power in that respect or, if no deputy has that power, by that court.

(2) A requirement or consent made or given under this Schedule by a surviving spouse or civil partner who is an infant shall be as valid and binding as it would be if he or she were of age, and, as respects an appropriation in pursuance of paragraph 1 of this Schedule, the provisions of section forty-one of the principal Act as to obtaining the consent of the infant's parent or guardian, or of the court on behalf of the infant, shall not apply.

7 (1) Except where the context otherwise requires, references in this Schedule to a dwelling-house include references to any garden or portion of ground attached to and usually occupied with the dwelling-house or otherwise required for the amenity or convenience of the dwelling-house.

(2) This Schedule shall be construed as one with Part IV of the principal Act.

APPENDIX A8

Wills Act 1837 extracts

9   Signing and attestation of wills

No will shall be valid unless–

(a)   it is in writing, and signed by the testator, or by some other person in his presence and by his direction; and

(b)   it appears that the testator intended by his signature to give effect to the will; and

(c)   the signature is made or acknowledged by the testator in the presence of two or more witnesses present at the same time; and

(d)   each witness either–

(i)   attests and signs the will; or

(ii)   acknowledges his signature, in the presence of the testator (but not necessarily in the presence of any other witness),

but no form of attestation shall be necessary.

15   Gifts to an attesting witness, or his or her wife or husband, to be void

If any person shall attest the execution of any will to whom or to whose wife or husband any beneficial devise, legacy, estate, interest, gift, or appointment, of or affecting any real or personal estate (other than and except charges and directions for the payment of any debt or debts), shall be thereby given or made, such devise, legacy, estate, interest, gift, or appointment shall, so far only as concerns such person attesting the execution of such will, or the wife or husband of such person, or any person claiming under such person or wife or husband, be utterly null and void, and such person so attesting shall be admitted as a witness to prove the execution of such will, or to prove the validity or invalidity thereof, notwithstanding such devise, legacy, estate, interest, gift, or appointment mentioned in such will.

18   Will to be revoked by marriage

(1)   Subject to subsections (2) to (4) below, a will shall be revoked by the testator's marriage.

(2)   A disposition in a will in exercise of a power of appointment shall take effect notwithstanding the testator's subsequent marriage unless the property so appointed would in default of appointment pass to his personal representatives.

(3)   Where it appears from a will that at the time it was made the testator was expecting to be married to a particular person and that he intended that the will should not be revoked by the marriage, the will shall not be revoked by his marriage to that person.

(4)   Where it appears from a will that at the time it was made the testator was expecting to be married to a particular person and that he intended that a disposition in the will should not be revoked by his marriage to that person,–

(a)   that disposition shall take effect notwithstanding the marriage; and

(b)   any other disposition in the will shall take effect also, unless it appears from the will that the testator intended the disposition to be revoked by the marriage.

18A Effect of dissolution or annulment of marriage on wills

(1) Where, after a testator has made a will, an order or decree of a court of civil jurisdiction in England and Wales dissolves or annuls his marriages or his marriage is dissolved or annulled and the divorce or annulment is entitled to recognition in England and Wales by virtue of Part II of the Family Law Act 1986,–

(a) provisions of the will appointing executors or trustees or conferring a power of appointment, if they appoint or confer the power on the former spouse, shall take effect as if the former spouse had died on the date on which the marriage is dissolved or annulled, and

(b) any property which, or an interest in which, is devised or bequeathed to the former spouse shall pass as if the former spouse had died on that date,

except in so far as a contrary intention appears by the will.

(2) Subsection (1)(b) above is without prejudice to any right of the former spouse to apply for financial provision under the Inheritance (Provision for Family and Dependants) Act 1975.

(3) [*repealed*]

18B Will to be revoked by civil partnership

(1) Subject to subsections (2) to (6), a will is revoked by the formation of a civil partnership between the testator and another person.

(2) A disposition in a will in exercise of a power of appointment takes effect despite the formation of a subsequent civil partnership between the testator and another person unless the property so appointed would in default of appointment pass to the testator's personal representatives.

(3) If it appears from a will–

(a) that at the time it was made the testator was expecting to form a civil partnership with a particular person, and

(b) that he intended that the will should not be revoked by the formation of the civil partnership,

the will is not revoked by its formation.

(4) Subsections (5) and (6) apply if it appears from a will–

(a) that at the time it was made the testator was expecting to form a civil partnership with a particular person, and

(b) that he intended that a disposition in the will should not be revoked by the formation of the civil partnership.

(5) The disposition takes effect despite the formation of the civil partnership.

(6) Any other disposition in the will also takes effect, unless it appears from the will that the testator intended the disposition to be revoked by the formation of the civil partnership.

20 No will to be revoked otherwise than as aforesaid or by another will or codicil, or by destruction thereof

No will or codicil, or any part thereof, shall be revoked otherwise than as aforesaid, or by another will or codicil executed in manner herein-before required, or by some writing declaring an intention to revoke the same and executed in the manner in which a will is herein-before required to be executed, or by the burning, tearing, or otherwise destroying the same by the testator, or by some person in his presence and by his direction, with the intention of revoking the same.

21   No alteration in a will after execution except in certain cases, shall have any effect unless executed as a will

No obliteration, interlineation, or other alteration made in any will after the execution thereof shall be valid or have any effect, except so far as the words or effect of the will before such alteration shall not be apparent, unless such alteration shall be executed in like manner as herein-before is required for the execution of the will; but the will, with such alteration as part thereof, shall be deemed to be duly executed if the signature of the testator and the subscription of the witnesses be made in the margin or on some other part of the will opposite or near to such alteration, or at the foot or end of or opposite to a memorandum referring to such alteration, and written at the end of some other part of the will.

24   Wills shall be construed, as to the estate comprised, to speak from the death of the testator

Every will shall be construed, with reference to the real estate and personal estate comprised in it, to speak and take effect as if it had been executed immediately before the death of the testator, unless a contrary intention shall appear by the will.

33   Gifts to children or other issue who leave issue living at the testator's death shall not lapse

(1)   Where–

    (a)   a will contains a devise or bequest to a child or remoter descendant of the testator; and

    (b)   the intended beneficiary dies before the testator, leaving issue; and

    (c)   issue of the intended beneficiary are living at the testator's death,

then, unless a contrary intention appears by the will, the devise or bequest shall take effect as a devise or bequest to the issue living at the testator's death.

(2)   Where–

    (a)   a will contains a devise or bequest to a class of person consisting of children or remoter descendants of the testator; and

    (b)   a member of the class dies before the testator, leaving issue, and

    (c)   issue of that member are living at the testator's death,

then, unless a contrary intention appears by the will, the devise or bequest shall take effect as if the class included the issue of its deceased member living at the testator's death.

(3)   Issue shall take under this section through all degrees, according to their stock, in equal shares if more than one, any gift or share which their parent would have taken and so that (subject to section 33A) no issue shall take whose parent is living at the testator's death and so capable of taking.

(4)   For the purposes of this section–

    (a)   the illegitimacy of any person is to be disregarded; and

    (b)   a person conceived before the testator's death and born living thereafter is to be taken to have been living at the testator's death.

33A   Disclaimer or forfeiture of gift

(1)   This section applies where a will contains a devise or bequest to a person who–

    (a)   disclaims it, or

(b)   has been precluded by the forfeiture rule from acquiring it.

(2)   The person is, unless a contrary intention appears by the will, to be treated for the purposes of this Act as having died immediately before the testator.

(3)   But in a case within subsection (1)(b), subsection (2) does not affect the power conferred by section 2 of the Forfeiture Act 1982 (power of court to modify the forfeiture rule).

(4)   In this section 'forfeiture rule' has the same meaning as in the Forfeiture Act 1982.

Appointment of a professional executor practice note

6 October 2011

1   INTRODUCTION

1.1   Who should read this practice note?

This practice note is for solicitors and law firms who provide will writing and probate services, and for solicitors and firms who are retained by, or have an economic relationship with a third party selling its own executor services, for example a solicitor or firm working with a high street bank that sells professional executor services.

1.2   What is the issue?

Clients who are considering the appointment of a solicitor or firm as executor(s) must be provided, by the potential executor(s), with sufficient information to make an informed decision about the appointment and its related costs.

Clients should be aware of the choice available for using either a professional or lay person when appointing an executor, and that if a lay person is appointed he or she may engage the services of a professional to assist with the administration of the estate on the death of the client

These requirements apply to all methods of Will writing services, including face-to-face, online and postal packs.

1.3   Professional conduct

The following sections of the SRA Code are relevant to this issue:

*   Chapter 1 on Client care
*   Chapter 4 on Confidentiality and disclosure

1.4   Status of this practice note

Practice notes are issued by the Law Society for the use and benefit of its members. They represent the Law Society's view of good practice in a particular area. They are not intended to be the only standard of good practice that solicitors can follow. You are not required to follow them, but doing so will make it easier to account to oversight bodies for your actions.

Practice notes are not legal advice, nor do they necessarily provide a defence to complaints of misconduct or of inadequate professional service. While care has been taken to ensure that they are accurate, up to date and useful, the Law Society will not accept any legal liability in relation to them.

For queries or comments on this practice note contact the Law Society's Practice Advice Service.

1.5   Terminology in this practice note

Must – A specific requirement in legislation or of a principle, rule, outcome or other mandatory provision in the SRA Handbook. You must comply, unless there are specific exemptions or defences provided for in relevant legislation or the SRA Handbook.

Should –

- Outside of a regulatory context, good practice for most situations in the Law Society's view.
- In the case of the SRA Handbook, an indicative behaviour or other non-mandatory provision (such as may be set out in notes or guidance).

These may not be the only means of complying with legislative or regulatory requirements and there may be situations where the suggested route is not the best possible route to meet the needs of your client. However, if you do not follow the suggested route, you should be able to justify to oversight bodies why the alternative approach you have taken is appropriate, either for your practice, or in the particular retainer.

May – A non-exhaustive list of options for meeting your obligations or running your practice. Which option you choose is determined by the profile of the individual practice, client or retainer. You may be required to justify why this was an appropriate option to oversight bodies.

SRA Code – SRA Code of Conduct 2011

SRA – Solicitors Regulation Authority

outcome – outcome

IB – indicative behaviour

2   SRA PRINCIPLES

There are ten mandatory principles which apply to all those the SRA regulates and to all aspects of practice. The principles can be found in the SRA Handbook.

The principles apply to solicitors or managers of authorised bodies who are practising from an office outside the UK. They also apply if you are a lawyer-controlled body practising from an office outside the UK.

3   APPOINTING AN EXECUTOR

When a client is considering the appointment of an executor, you may promote you or your firm's services as an executor, but you should inform the client that such appointment is not compulsory, and you should take into account the size and complexity of the estate before promoting you or your firm's services instead of a lay executor.

You should inform the client that an executor can be either a:

1.   professional such as you or your firm, or
2.   lay person(s) such as a family member or beneficiary, who has the option of engaging a professional to assist him or her in the administration of the estate.

If you decide to promote your services you should also take into account the client's best interests. For example, if the estate is small or straightforward, it may not be appropriate to encourage the client to appoint you or your firm as the executor.

Before finalising a Will that appoints you or your firm as an executor(s) you should therefore be satisfied that:

1.   the client understands that the executor does not have to be a professional and that a lay person(s) such as a family member or beneficiary can be appointed and that lay person(s) have the option of engaging professional help after the client's death, if they require assistance, and

2.   it is not contrary to the client's best interests at the time of drafting the Will to make such an appointment.

For further information see the Solicitors Regulation Authority's guidance on Drafting wills which appoint you or your firm as executor(s).

4   PROVIDING INFORMATION ABOUT EXECUTOR FEES

If a client is considering naming you or your firm as an executor you should provide an indication of the likely current costs of both:

1.   carrying out the administration of the estate, and
2.   acting as an executor.

You should also inform the client whether the fees quoted are based on:

1.   an hourly rate, and/or
2.   a percentage of the estate.

It should be clear whether the amount quoted is for the work involved in administering the estate or whether it is simply the fee for acting as an executor and supervising others doing the necessary work.

With some executorships there may be a continuing role for you as executor to act as a trustee. In these cases you should make clear any trustee fees that may be relevant to the estate.

Information about fees should be provided upfront so that the client is made aware of potential charges before deciding who to appoint. You should also ensure your client understands that these fees may change in the future.

If your services are being provided online or through the post it is important that your fees are clearly and prominently presented in any information provided to the client before the client elects to appoint you or your firm as the executor(s).

5   RENOUNCING PROBATE

In some cases where you have been appointed as an executor(s) you may be asked by the beneficiaries to renounce probate on the death of your client. You are not required to do so.

If you choose to consider such a request you should look at the reasons you or your firm were appointed as executor(s). If you are both executor and trustee, you should consider whether it is appropriate to disclaim your trusteeship as well as renouncing your executorship, as the two roles are different.

You should also consider whether, at the date of death, circumstances have changed from the time the client appointed you or your firm, and what is now in the best interests of the estate, including whether the administration of the estate could easily be handled by a lay executor.

Further guidance is available from the SRA.

6 FURTHER INFORMATION

6.1 Practice advice

6.1.1 Practice Advice Service

The Law Society provides support to solicitors on a wide range of areas of legal practice. The Practice Advice Service is staffed by solicitors and can be contacted on 0870 606 2522 from 09.00 to 17.00 on weekdays.

6.1.2 Solicitors Regulation Authority

The SRA's Question of Ethics web pages provides practical guidance on this issue.

6.2 Acknowledgements

The Law Society wishes to thank members of the Wills and Equity Committee for their assistance in drafting this practice note.

Bankrupt beneficiaries practice note

15 September 2011

1 INTRODUCTION

1.1 Who should read this practice note?

Managing partners, probate practitioners and other practice staff involved in:

- obtaining grants of representation of estates; or
- the administration of estates; or
- advising personal representatives.

1.2 What is the issue?

Personal representatives who make a distribution out of the estate of a deceased person to a bankrupt beneficiary may be making the distribution to the wrong person, and, if so, will not receive a good receipt.

In such cases, if the bankrupt puts the assets beyond the reach of the trustee in bankruptcy, there is a real risk that the trustee in bankruptcy, on behalf of the bankrupt's creditors, will claim compensation against the personal representatives.

The claim would be equal to either:

- the amount of the payment to the bankrupt; or
- the value of the assets transferred to the bankrupt.

Where personal representatives have wrongly distributed assets to a person who was or is an undischarged bankrupt, it may be difficult for the personal representatives to succeed in a claim to recover those assets because of the restrictions placed upon bringing proceedings against bankrupts by section 285 of the Insolvency Act 1986.

This practice note provides advice for practitioners acting under these circumstances.

1.3 Status of this practice note

Practice notes are issued by the Law Society for the use and benefit of its members. They represent the Law Society's view of good practice in a particular area. They are not intended to be the only standard of good practice that solicitors can follow. You are not required to follow them, but doing so will make it easier to account to oversight bodies for your actions.

Practice notes are not legal advice, nor do they necessarily provide a defence to complaints of misconduct or of inadequate professional service. While care has been taken to ensure that they are accurate, up to date and useful, the Law Society will not accept any legal liability in relation to them.

For queries or comments on this practice note contact the Law Society's Practice Advice Service.

1.4 Terminology in this practice note

Must – A specific requirement in legislation or of a principle, rule, outcome or other mandatory provision in the SRA Handbook. You must comply, unless there are specific exemptions or defences provided for in relevant legislation or the SRA Handbook.

Should

- Outside of a regulatory context, good practice for most situations in the Law Society's view.
- In the case of the SRA Handbook, an indicative behaviour or other non-mandatory provision (such as may be set out in notes or guidance).

These may not be the only means of complying with legislative or regulatory requirements and there may be situations where the suggested route is not the best possible route to meet the needs of your client. However, if you do not follow the suggested route, you should be able to justify to oversight bodies why the alternative approach you have taken is appropriate, either for your practice, or in the particular retainer.

May – A non-exhaustive list of options for meeting your obligations or running your practice. Which option you choose is determined by the profile of the individual practice, client or retainer. You may be required to justify why this was an appropriate option to oversight bodies.

2 BASIS OF A CLAIM BY A TRUSTEE IN BANKRUPTCY TO THE INHERITANCE OF THE BANKRUPT BENEFICIARY

When a trustee in bankruptcy is appointed, all property (which is defined very widely in section 436 of the Insolvency Act 1986) belonging to the bankrupt automatically vests in the trustee in bankruptcy: section 306 of the Insolvency Act 1986. The statutory definition of 'property' includes 'things in action'.

The benefit of this asset vests in the trustee in bankruptcy in the same way as other assets of the bankrupt.

The recent decision in *Re Bertha Hemming Deceased, Raymond Saul & Co.* v *Holden* [2008] EWHC 2731 (Ch) confirms that in such cases the 'thing in action' which vests in the trustee in bankruptcy is a composite right made up of:

- the right to have the estate administered; and
- the right to have the assets comprised in the distribution paid over or transferred at the conclusion of the administration of the estate.

2.1 Death occurring before bankruptcy

A beneficiary who, at the date when the bankruptcy order is made, is entitled to undistributed property under the will or on the intestacy of a deceased person is entitled to a 'thing in action', namely, the right to compel the due administration of the estate.

It makes no difference whether the assets are in the form of money, chattels, or other property. It is the trustee in bankruptcy who is entitled to receive the assets comprised in the distribution under the will or on the intestacy of the deceased, and not the beneficiary.

The trustee in bankruptcy's right to receive the assets is not affected by the subsequent discharge of the bankrupt beneficiary from bankruptcy. In these cases, the 'thing in action' vests in the trustee in bankruptcy under section 306 of the Insolvency Act 1986 at the time of the bankruptcy, and the question of after-acquired property does not arise.

2.2   Death occurring after bankruptcy

A beneficiary who remains the subject of a bankruptcy order may become entitled as a beneficiary to an interest in property passing under the will or intestacy of a deceased person.

In such cases, the 'thing in action' (ie the composite right to have the estate administered, and the right to have the assets comprised in the distribution paid over at the conclusion of the administration of the estate) constitutes 'after-acquired property' (see section 307 of the Insolvency Act 1986).

After-acquired property vests, in the first place, in the bankrupt.

2.2.1   Giving notice to the trustee in bankruptcy

Section 333 of the Insolvency Act 1986 requires the bankrupt to give notice to the trustee in bankruptcy of any property which devolves upon him or her of which he or she has acquired or any increase in income, since the commencement of the bankruptcy, within 21 days of the devolution, acquisition or increase.

A failure by the bankrupt to meet this obligation is punishable as a contempt of court, section 333(4) of the Insolvency Act 1986.

The trustee in bankruptcy may then claim such 'after-acquired property' by either:

- serving notice on the bankrupt within 42 days of first becoming aware of the devolution, acquisition or increase; or,
- serving such notice on the bankrupt after 42 days from first becoming aware of the acquisition, but only with the permission of the court.

See section 307(1) of the Insolvency Act 1986.

The trustee in bankruptcy is entitled to after-acquired property only after he or she has served such notice.

See also *Vickers* v *Mitchell* [2004] All ER (D) 414 and *Solomon* v *Williams* [2001] All ER (D) 299 as to the effect of failure by the trustee in bankruptcy to serve the section 307(1) notice promptly.

Where the personal representatives are aware that the beneficiary became bankrupt before the time of the deceased's death, they can, before making any distribution to the bankrupt, properly insist on seeing the notice regarding the after-acquired property constituted by the interest in the deceased's estate which the bankrupt is required by section 333(2) of the Insolvency Act 1986 to give to the trustee in bankruptcy.

Having been provided with such notice, the personal representatives would then need to confirm with the trustee in bankruptcy whether the trustee in bankruptcy had served a notice on the bankrupt under section 307(1) of the Insolvency Act 1986, or intended to serve such a notice.

If the trustee in bankruptcy had served a section 307(1) notice, or intended to do so and did so, within the time allowed, then the personal representatives could properly distribute the property only to the trustee in bankruptcy. The trustee in bankruptcy could then give the personal representatives a good receipt.

If (unusually) the trustee in bankruptcy had not served, and did not intend to serve, a notice under section 307(1), then the personal representatives could properly distribute the property to the bankrupt and the bankrupt could give the personal representatives a good receipt.

The trustee in bankruptcy has no claim only where the bankrupt has already been discharged at the time of death of the testator or the intestate under whose estate the former bankrupt benefits.

2.2.2   *If the personal representatives are uncertain of the beneficiary's status*

Whilst the position of personal representatives who are aware that the beneficiary has been made bankrupt may be relatively straightforward, the position is more difficult if they are unsure whether the beneficiary is bankrupt.

In relation to after-acquired property, section 307(4) of the Insolvency Act 1986 now makes clear that, whether before or after service of a notice under section 307(1), where a person acquires property in good faith, for value and without notice of the bankruptcy, the trustee in bankruptcy is not entitled to any remedy against that person, or against any person whose title to the property derives from that person.

If the beneficiary has been made bankrupt, section 307(4) does not protect the personal representatives, who have not 'acquired' the relevant property but transferred it to the beneficiary.

The transfer by the personal representatives will not have been made for value, but under a purported legal obligation to the beneficiary. In the absence of protection from section 307(4) personal representatives who wrongly transfer property to a bankrupt beneficiary, will not obtain a good receipt.

If the bankrupt succeeds in putting the assets out of reach of the trustee in bankruptcy, the personal representatives will risk facing a claim for compensation by the trustee in bankruptcy, to whom the distribution should have been made.

The enactment of section 307(4) means that you can no longer rely on previous authorities which state that someone dealing in good faith with a bankrupt and without notice of the bankruptcy cannot be sued by the trustee in bankruptcy to recover the value of after-acquired property transferred to the bankrupt.

3   OBTAINING INFORMATION ABOUT THE BENEFICIARY

The personal representatives may directly ask a beneficiary whether they are, or ever have been, bankrupt. However the beneficiary may provide misleading information or false information or even refuse to answer the question. It is therefore risky to rely on information gained in this way without carrying out further investigations.

The personal representatives may ask a beneficiary to provide details and evidence (in the form of copies of birth or marriage certificates, or deeds poll) of his or her true names and of any other versions of names the beneficiary uses.

3.1   Obtaining full disclosure

If a bankrupt knowingly fails to disclose to his or her trustee in bankruptcy all the property, books, papers and records forming his or her estate or relevant disposals of such property, he or she will be committing a criminal offence: section 353(1) and (2) of the Insolvency Act 1986.

A bankrupt is also required by section 333(2) of the Insolvency Act 1986 to give notice to the trustee in bankruptcy of any after-acquired property to which he or she becomes entitled while his or her bankruptcy remains undischarged.

Further, the bankrupt will be guilty of a criminal offence if he or she causes the making of false entries in or omissions from any book, document or records relating to his or her affairs: section 355(2)(c) and (3)(a) of the Insolvency Act 1986.

All of the above offences are punishable by a fine, imprisonment, or both: section 350(6) of the Insolvency Act 1986.

You may wish to consider drawing these offences to the attention of beneficiaries before questioning them as to their affairs.

If the bankrupt complies with his or her legal obligations, the trustee in bankruptcy will ordinarily notify the personal representatives that any distribution from the deceased's estate should be made to the trustee in bankruptcy, and not to the bankrupt, and that the personal representatives can safely make the distribution and get a good receipt where:

- the bankruptcy order was made before the date of the deceased's death and the trustee in bankruptcy has provided evidence that he or she has served a s307(1) notice on the bankrupt; or
- the bankruptcy order was made after the date of the deceased's death.

Where the personal representatives know that the beneficiary is a bankrupt, the personal representatives should contact the trustee in bankruptcy before making any distribution in order to obtain confirmation that the proposed distribution will be made to the person entitled in law to receive it.

In all other cases, the personal representatives should, before making a distribution to any beneficiary in England and Wales, carry out a bankruptcy-only search at the Land Charges Department of Her Majesty's Land Registry against the name of each beneficiary to whom it is proposed to make a distribution.

3.2 Conducting bankruptcy searches

Immediately after a bankruptcy petition has been filed, the court must apply to the Land Charges Department to register the petition against the name of the respondent in the register of pending actions under section 5(1)(b) of the Land Charges Act 1972.

Immediately after the court has made a bankruptcy order, the Official Receiver must apply to register it against the name of the bankrupt in the register of writs and orders under section 6(1) of the Land Charges Act 1972.

Searches carried out at the Land Charges Department will be able to establish whether, within the previous five years, the beneficiary was subject to a bankruptcy order, unless a court order cancelling the registration has been made.

The search can be conducted online or by using Form K16. The current fee is £2 per search against each name. This can be charged as an administration cost against the residue of the estate.

3.2.1 Period of effective registration in the Land Charges Department

Registration in the Land Charges Department remains effective for a period of five years: section 8 of the Land Charges Act 1972, but then ceases to have effect unless it is renewed.

You should be aware that the discharge of the bankrupt from bankruptcy does not cause the registration to be cancelled, unless a court makes an order cancelling the registration.

There is therefore an element of risk in any case in which the administration of an estate has taken five years or more before the making of any distributions, or if an order has been made cancelling the registration before the end of the five year period.

3.2.2 Other information services

The Insolvency Service retains details of all bankruptcies in England and Wales which are current, or which have terminated within the previous three months.

Section 279(1) of the Insolvency Act 1986 provides that a bankrupt is discharged from bankruptcy at the end of the period of one year starting with the commencement of the bankruptcy. The trustee may however apply to the court for an order that the specified period of one year should cease to run, on the grounds that the undischarged bankrupt has failed or is failing to comply with an obligation under his or her bankruptcy.

You should note that searching at the Land Registry is more likely to produce relevant information about a bankrupt beneficiary than searching at the Insolvency Service because an entry at the Land Registry will, unless a court otherwise orders, remain on the register for a period of five years after it was first made.

Therefore, except in cases where the court has ordered that the specified period of a year should be substantially extended, a Land Registry search is likely to be the better option.

3.3 Searching against the correct name

Personal representatives may have to carry out more than one search in respect of a single beneficiary in case they are known under more than one name, or one spelling of a name. Searches should therefore be conducted against:

- the name of the beneficiary as shown on any relevant will;
- the full name of the beneficiary both with and without any name by which he or she is or has been generally known;
- the first forename and family name of the beneficiary.

You should note that the search process recognises only exact matches and cannot be relied upon where spelling errors have been made.

3.4 Conducting a search at the correct time

A search should be made immediately before making a distribution to a beneficiary, since earlier searches will not reveal a bankruptcy petition filed, or a bankruptcy order made between the search and the date of the distribution.

Example

Ted died on 5 January 2009. He left half of the residue of his estate to his nephew, Ben. Ben was declared bankrupt on 12 January 2009, and received his automatic discharge on 12 January 2010. Ted's personal representative was in a position to distribute the residue of Ted's estate in May 2010. Because Ben's bankruptcy was discharged in January 2010, the Insolvency Service will have ceased to record it in April 2010. However, a search at the Land Registry will, unless a court makes a contrary order, continue to disclose that Ben was made bankrupt until January 2014.

If a Land Registry search provides a positive result, it may be sensible to carry out an Insolvency Service search as well as this will disclose the identity of the court dealing with the relevant bankruptcy and the case number.

3.5 Acting on the search results

Where the searches reveal no entry in the appropriate register and the personal representatives have no knowledge of the beneficiary's bankruptcy, it is safe to proceed with making the distribution.

The fact that a beneficiary is known to have substantial debts is not a reason for not making a distribution to which he or she is entitled.

If the bankruptcy search reveals that a bankruptcy petition has been served, but no bankruptcy order has yet been made, then it is unsafe for the personal representatives to make a distribution to the beneficiary unless the bankruptcy petition is dismissed.

Under section 284(1) of the Insolvency Act 1986 any disposition of property made by a bankrupt is void unless it was made by consent of the court or subsequently ratified by the court.

This applies from the date of the presentation of the bankruptcy petition until the vesting of the bankrupt's estate in the trustee in bankruptcy: section 284(3).

The personal representatives should therefore always await the outcome of the hearing of the bankruptcy petition before making any distribution.

If a search reveals that a bankruptcy order has been made before or after the date of death of the deceased, then personal representatives cannot safely make any payment to the beneficiary, even if the bankruptcy has been discharged by the time of the proposed payment.

Only if the bankruptcy is annulled and all the bankruptcy search entries are removed is it safe for the personal representatives to make a payment to the beneficiary.

If, however, the death of the deceased occurs only after the date of discharge of the bankrupt beneficiary, and the beneficiary is not subsequently made bankrupt again, then the personal representatives, having made the appropriate searches, may safely make a distribution to the discharged bankrupt.

Discharge from bankruptcy means that the discharged bankrupt may again acquire and dispose of property on his or her own account.

4   MAKING PAYMENTS

Personal representatives are not obliged to comply with unusual requests for payment by a beneficiary, for example, into an account maintained offshore, or into an account in the name of a third party in circumstances that suggest an intention to improperly divert the funds from the trustee in bankruptcy.

Personal representatives should consider declining such requests in order to reduce the risk of exposing themselves to a claim by the trustee in bankruptcy.

If personal representatives are uncertain whether to make payment to one or other of two parties they may apply for directions to court. If they act reasonably in doing so and have not made such application for their own benefit, they should not have to bear the costs of such an application personally. But if the court determines that the answer is clear, and the application was unnecessary, the personal representatives may be ordered to pay for the costs personally.

If the personal representatives do not maintain a neutral position in the application but advance a particular case which is unsuccessful, they are at risk of being ordered to pay the successful party's costs: *Re Bertha Hemming Deceased, Raymond Saul & Co. v Holden* [2008] EWHC 8565 (Ch).

If personal representatives are unsure as to whom they should make a payment, they may, as a last resort pay the funds in question into court under section 63 of the Trustee Act 1925. Again, there is a potential risk of an adverse costs order if the court determines that there was no obvious uncertainty and that the payment into court was unnecessary.

The procedure for paying funds into court is set out in the Civil Procedure Rules Practice Direction 37 paragraph 6.

See also the Civil Procedure Rules Practice Direction 37 paragraphs 3 and 7 for the procedure for applying for payment out of funds held by the court.

5   INDIVIDUAL VOLUNTARY ARRANGEMENTS

Individual voluntary arrangements (IVAs) may in some cases, avoid a debtor being adjudicated bankrupt, but the law also allows debtors to submit proposals for an IVA after a bankruptcy order has been made. The details of any particular IVA has to be considered before a decision can be made about the correct person to whom the personal representatives should make a payment.

In an IVA case in which a bankruptcy petition has been presented and a bankruptcy order made, sections 306 and 307 of the Insolvency Act 1986 apply, and personal representatives remain at risk if they make payment to the wrong party.

In general, for IVA cases in which no bankruptcy petition has been presented, or in which a petition has been presented but has been dismissed at the time when the distribution is made, the existence of the IVA will not affect the beneficiary's right to receive the payment and give a good receipt.

Under an IVA made between the debtor, the creditors and the supervisor of the IVA, the debtor usually covenants to disclose any windfall which he or she may receive to the trustee of the IVA, but sections 306 and 307 of the Insolvency Act 1986 do not apply where no bankruptcy petition has been presented or the petition has been dismissed and no bankruptcy order is made.

6   INTERNATIONAL BANKRUPTCIES

If a beneficiary who is, or who becomes, bankrupt is based outside England and Wales, the rules of English law set out above may not apply. Lawyers qualified in England and Wales are not competent to advise on bankruptcies governed by the law of other jurisdictions.

Therefore, a personal representative may have to seek legal advice from an insolvency lawyer who is qualified in the jurisdiction in which a beneficiary has his or her centre of main interests or is otherwise subject to insolvency proceedings.

6.1   Vesting rules and after-acquired property rules outside England and Wales

6.1.1   *Beneficiary based in the UK*

If the relevant beneficiary or bankrupt beneficiary has his centre of main interests (COMI) in the UK or in another EU State (other than Denmark), Council Regulation (EC) No 1346/2000 of 29 May 2000 on Insolvency Proceedings (the EC Regulation) will apply. The COMI of a company or individual must be identified by reference to factors that are both objective and ascertainable by third parties.

According to Article 3(1) of the EC Regulation, if the COMI of a beneficiary is in the UK, the relevant courts of England and Wales, Scotland or Northern Ireland will have jurisdiction in respect of the opening by a creditor of bankruptcy proceedings and the relevant part of UK law will apply: see Article 3(1) of the EC Regulation.

If the beneficiary has already been made bankrupt in the UK, the relevant law of the UK will apply to his or her bankruptcy.

The treatment of beneficiaries who are based in England and Wales is different to that of beneficiaries based in Scotland or Northern Ireland.

6.1.2   *The relevant UK jurisdiction*

If the EC Regulation is applicable and the COMI of the beneficiary is in the UK, in order for the courts of England and Wales to have jurisdiction, it must be established that one of the criteria in section 265 of the Insolvency Act 1986 is applicable, ie that the debtor is:

- domiciled in England and Wales;
- is present in England and Wales on the day the petition is presented; or
- in the three years ending with that day was ordinarily resident or carried out a business in England and Wales.

If the beneficiary does not fall within any of the section 265 criteria (ie they are based in Scotland or Northern Ireland), any bankruptcy proceedings by a creditor must be commenced in the relevant part of the UK where the required nexus exists.

The rules that apply to both the vesting of property in the trustees in bankruptcy and to after-acquired property are likely to be the rules of the part of the UK in which the bankruptcy order was made.

The personal representatives should therefore take advice from a lawyer with expertise in the law of that part of the UK, as to the vesting rules and how the after-acquired property rules work within that jurisdiction before making a distribution out of the estate.

6.1.3 *Beneficiary based in another EU Member State (except Denmark)*

Where a beneficiary has his COMI in another Member State within the EU (except Denmark, until such time as it signs up to the EC Regulation), the courts of England and Wales must refuse jurisdiction to open main bankruptcy proceedings in England or Wales, unless the beneficiary has an establishment in England or Wales, as defined in Article 2(h) of the EC Regulation. The appropriate course of action for a creditor would usually be to take proceedings to make the individual bankrupt in the Member State in which he or she has his or her COMI.

The law of the Member State in which insolvency proceedings are opened should be the applicable law: see Article 4 of the EC Regulation. The proceedings are opened at the time of the court order, ie the date of the bankruptcy order for individuals. Therefore, where a beneficiary has his or her COMI in another EU Member State and is made bankrupt there, the law that will be applied to his or her bankruptcy is likely to be the law of that Member State.

The rules relating to the vesting of property in the trustee and relating to after-acquired property that are applied are likely to be the rules of the Member State in which the bankruptcy order was made.

Again, the personal representatives should take advice from a foreign lawyer within that jurisdiction as to the vesting rules and how the after-acquired property rules work within that jurisdiction before making a distribution out of the estate.

6.1.4 *Beneficiary based outside the EU or in Denmark*

In cases where a beneficiary is based outside of the EU or in Denmark, the EC Regulation does not apply to the determination of what is the applicable law for the opening of bankruptcy proceedings.

Where the EC Regulation does not apply, the relevant country is free to apply its national laws of jurisdiction, choice of law and recognition and enforcement of judgments.

If a bankrupt or potential bankrupt is resident in and/or may have a COMI in another jurisdiction outside the EU (or in Denmark), the personal representatives should take advice from a lawyer in that country as to:

1. the jurisdiction of their courts; and
2. the laws regarding the vesting of property in the trustee in bankruptcy and the after-acquired property laws in respect of bankruptcy within that jurisdiction.

If the courts of England or Wales take jurisdiction in respect of a beneficiary with a connection to England or Wales pursuant to section 265 of the Insolvency Act 1986 in a situation where the beneficiary has connections to other foreign jurisdictions, the beneficiary may become subject to bankruptcy proceedings in more than one jurisdiction, especially where their assets are located in multiple jurisdictions.

6.2   Recognition and enforcement of judgments in the English and Wales courts

Personal representatives should be aware that judgments of courts outside of England and Wales relating to insolvency law will be recognised and enforced by the courts of England and Wales.

6.2.1 Judgments from other parts of the UK

An order made by a court in any part of the UK in the exercise of jurisdiction in relation to insolvency law shall be enforced in any other part of the UK (ie Scotland or Northern Ireland) as if it were made by a court exercising the corresponding jurisdiction in that other part (save for orders relating to property situated in that part): see section 426 of the Insolvency Act 1986.

6.2.2 Judgments from other EU Countries (except Denmark)

Any judgment opening insolvency main proceedings handed down by a court of a Member State which has jurisdiction pursuant to Article 3 of the EC Regulation will be recognised in all other Member States (ie a judgment making a person bankrupt in France will be recognised in all other Member States, the authority of the French trustee in bankruptcy will be similarly recognised and consequently French law will apply to the bankruptcy: see Article 4, Article 16 and Article 18 of the EC Regulation).

6.2.3 Judgments from countries outside the EU and Denmark

The recognition of bankruptcies which have been opened outside of the UK will be governed by:

* The Cross-Border Insolvency Regulations 2006 (2006/1030); or
* The common law principles of English law; and/or
* Section 426 of the Insolvency Act 1986.

7 MORE INFORMATION

7.1 References

7.1.1 Legal and statutory regulations

* Civil Procedure Rules Practice Direction 37
* Insolvency Act 1986
* Land Charges Act 1972
* Trustee Act 1925
* Council Regulation (EC) No 1346/2000 of 29 May 2000 on Insolvency Proceedings
* The Cross-Border Insolvency Regulations 2006 (2006/1030)

7.1.2 Cases

* *Re Bertha Hemming Deceased, Raymond Saul & Co.* v *Holden* [2008] EWHC 2731 (Ch)
* *Vickers* v *Mitchell* [2004] All ER (D) 414
* *Solomon* v *Williams* [2001] All ER (D) 299

7.2 Further products and support

7.2.1 Practice Advice Line

The Law Society provides support for solicitors on a wide range of areas of practice. Practice Advice can be contacted on 0870 606 2522 from 09:00 to 17:00 on weekdays.

7.2.2 Professional Ethics Helpline

Solicitors Regulation Authority's Professional Ethics Helpline for advice on conduct issues.

7.3 Acknowledgements

The Law Society wishes to thank members of the Wills & Equity Committee for their assistance in drafting this practice note.

Cancellation of contracts practice note

6 October 2011

1 INTRODUCTION

1.1 Who should read this practice note?

Solicitors who enter into contracts with clients, including conditional fee agreements or client care agreements, away from the solicitor's own place of business, or following discussions that take place away from their own place of business.

1.2 What is the issue?

The Cancellation of Contracts made in a Consumer's Home or Place of Work etc Regulations 2008 ('the Regulations') came into force on 1 October 2008.

The Regulations are likely to apply to a wide range of contracts made between solicitors and their clients. Whether they apply will depend on the nature of the client and the circumstances in which the contract was made.

Where the Regulations apply then the client has a right to cancel the contract within a 7 day period. The solicitor must give the client written notice of this right, setting out various prescribed information. Failure to do so is a criminal offence.

This practice note considers in what circumstances the Regulations will apply to contracts between solicitors and their clients, and explains the consequences if the Regulations apply.

1.3 Status of this practice note

Practice notes are issued by the Law Society for the use and benefit of its members. They represent the Law Society's view of good practice in a particular area. They are not intended to be the only standard of good practice that solicitors can follow. You are not required to follow them, but doing so will make it easier to account to oversight bodies for your actions.

Practice notes are not legal advice, nor do they necessarily provide a defence to complaints of misconduct or of inadequate professional service. While care has been taken to ensure that they are accurate, up to date and useful, the Law Society will not accept any legal liability in relation to them.

For queries or comments on this practice note, contact the Law Society's Practice Advice Service.

1.4 Terminology

Must – A specific requirement in legislation or of a principle, rule, outcome or other mandatory provision in the SRA Handbook. You must comply, unless there are specific exemptions or defences provided for in relevant legislation or the SRA Handbook.

Should –

- Outside of a regulatory context, good practice for most situations in the Law Society's view. In the case of the SRA Handbook, an indicative behaviour or other non-mandatory provision (such as may be set out in notes or guidance).
- These may not be the only means of complying with legislative or regulatory requirements and there may be situations where the suggested route is not the best possible route to meet the needs of your client. However, if you do not follow the suggested route, you should be able to justify to oversight bodies why the alternative approach you have taken is appropriate, either for your practice, or in the particular retainer.

May – A non-exhaustive list of options for meeting your obligations or running your practice. Which option you choose is determined by the profile of the individual practice, client or retainer. You may be required to justify why this was an appropriate option to oversight bodies.

2   THE REGULATIONS

The scope of the Regulations is governed by regulation 5. This provides that the Regulations apply to a contract between a consumer and a trader:

1.   which is for the supply of goods or services to the consumer by a trader and
2.   which is made:

   –   during a visit by the trader to the consumer's home or place of work, or to the home of another individual;
   –   during an excursion organised by the trader away from his business premises; or
   –   after an offer made by the consumer during such a visit or excursion.

Under regulation 5, the Regulations apply to contracts for the supply of goods or services to the consumer by a trader. Contracts for the provision of legal advice or other legal services would therefore come within the Regulations.

2.1   Regulation 2(1): Definitions

A solicitor entering into a contract with a client is a 'trader' within the meaning of the Regulations. A 'trader' is defined in regulation 2(1) as 'a person who, in making a contract to which these Regulations apply, is acting in his commercial or professional capacity and anyone acting in the name or on behalf of a trader'.

A 'consumer' is defined in regulation 2(1) as 'a natural person who in making a contract to which these Regulations apply is acting for purposes which can be regarded as outside his trade or profession'. So not all clients will be consumers; but many clients will be caught by the Regulations.

2.2   Regulation 6: Exemptions

Regulation 6 sets out a number of contracts to which the Regulations do not apply. Where your contract consists wholly of exempt activities, you will not be subject to the Regulations. As a brief summary, the exemptions relate to:

- a cancellable agreement
- consumer credit agreements
- certain contracts made after a solicited visit
- immovable property
- foodstuffs or beverages
- supply of goods or services based on a trader's catalogue

- insurance
- credit provided which does not exceed £35 other than a hire purchase or conditional sale agreement and
- regulated activity relating to investments.

In most cases, these exemptions are unlikely to be relevant to contracts between solicitors and their clients. However you must refer to Regulation 6 and Schedule 3 of the Regulations for the full list of exempt contracts.

Work undertaken on the basis of legal aid funding is not excluded, and may fall within the scope of the Regulations. Whether or not it will do so depends on the matters discussed in the next section. The relevant contract, for the purposes of the Regulations, would be between the consumer (ie the client) and the trader (ie the solicitor), notwithstanding that the solicitor receives payment from a third party funder. Thus where the Regulations apply written notice of the right to cancel must be provided to the client. Any legal aid client care letter should point out the potential difficulties in re-applying for legal aid for the same issue, if the contract is terminated. The Regulations do not affect the rights and liabilities of the solicitor and the funder under any separate funding agreement between them.

3   SITUATIONS IN WHICH THE REGULATIONS APPLY

The Regulations only apply if the contract is made in one of the three situations described in limbs (a)–(c) of Regulation 5. The following text describes how those provisions may apply as between a solicitor and their client.

3.1   First situation: contracts made in homes or workplaces

Limb (a) specifies situations in which the contract is made during a visit by the solicitor to:

- the client's home or place of work or
- the home of another individual.

Other than in respect of those agreements outside the scope of the regulations (see regulation 6), it does not matter whether the solicitor made the visit at the client's request; the relevant factor is whether the visit is to one of the places specified in (a), and whether the contract is made during that visit.

3.2   Second situation: contracts made during excursions

Limb (b) specifies situations in which the contract is made during an excursion organised by the solicitor away from their business premises.
   This only applies if:

- the contract was made during an excursion organised by the solicitor and
- the excursion was away from the solicitor's normal business premises.

For example, if a contract is made over dinner at a restaurant, and the meal was organised by your client, then limb (b) does not apply. However, if you organised the meal then limb (b) would apply.
   If the contract is made during a drinks party at your office then limb (b) would not apply; but if the drinks party took place at some other venue, and you organised it, limb (b) would apply.
   The precise scope of limb (b) is, however, unclear. Until it is clarified by case-law, it is prudent to assume that limb (b) would apply to any situation where a solicitor arranged to meet a client

away from his business premises. Therefore, if you arrange to meet a client in hospital you should assume that this falls within limb (b), even though the meeting would not be social in nature and the client and solicitor would not go anywhere or do anything together.

3.3 Distinguishing between situations 1 and 2

In order to determine whether the contract falls within (a) or (b), you must be aware of the point in time when a contract is made with your client. Difficult questions may arise where discussions take place with your client in your business office, either face to face or on the telephone, and then those discussions are continued during a visit falling within (a) or an excursion falling within (b). Determining when and where a contract was made will depend on the facts of the particular case.

In some cases it will be clear at which point the contract came into effect. For example, if a client telephones you and you orally run through the terms of the agreement and inform them of costs, and a client care letter is sent to the client with their agreement prior to any visit or excursion, then the situation would be unlikely to fall within (a) or (b). However, caution must be exercised if a subsequent agreement is made during a follow up visit; such an agreement may be a new contract, and caught by the Regulations. In general, where there is doubt you should assume that the Regulations do apply, to avoid criminal penalties for any breach.

3.4 Third situation: contracts made after a visit or excursion

Limb (c) of Regulation 5 will apply if the contract is made after an offer made by the consumer during:

- a visit (falling within limb (a)); or
- an excursion (falling within limb (b)).

A contract may fall within limb (c) even if it is made in your office, if it is made after an offer of the relevant kind made by the client.

For example, if you visit a client at home, the client offers to engage you to carry out legal work, and you then accept the offer by telephoning the client from your office the following day, then the Regulations will apply.

In order for limb (c) to apply, it is not necessary for the contract to be made by your acceptance of the client's offer. For instance, it may be that the client makes an offer, and that you subsequently make a counter-offer which the client accepts. In this case the contract would be made after the client's offer. However, if the client's offer was not part of the negotiations leading to the contract, but was a wholly separate matter, then limb (c) would be unlikely to apply.

For example: you visit a client at home and the client offers to engage you to perform work at an hourly rate of £80 but you refuse. After returning to your office you write a letter offering to do the work for £100 an hour, and the client accepts. The contract is made after an offer made by the client during a home visit: it therefore comes within (c) and the Regulations would apply.

If, however the client refuses your initial offer but telephones you at your office six months later to request that you do other work for £100 an hour, and you agree, the client's initial offer is wholly separate from the contract that has come into existence, and limb (c) is therefore unlikely to apply.

You should bear in mind that regulation 5(c) applies where a contract is made after an offer made by the consumer in certain circumstances. The word offer probably bears its normal contractual meaning; ie a communication that would be capable, if accepted, of giving rise to a binding contract. Not every request as to whether a solicitor would be willing to carry out work will be an offer in this sense.

3.5   In practice: determining where regulations apply

The following are hypothetical examples of how the Regulations may apply in practice:

Example 1

A client phones you and during this call you take oral instructions to prepare a Will for the client. You later visit the client's home with the drafted Will based on the oral instructions provided over the phone and the client signs the Will without any amendments.

In this situation the Regulations probably do not apply as the contract was probably made during the telephone conversation and prior to the visit. If however the contract did not come into existence until the visit itself then limb (a) of regulation 5 would apply, and the contract would come within the Regulations.

If the Will was subsequently amended during the visit to the client's home then this would probably make no difference to the above analysis. If the contract was made before the home visit, the work done in amending the Will will almost certainly fall within the scope of that contract, rather than being the subject of a fresh contract.

Example 2

A relative of one of your clients, acting on behalf of your client, visits your office and provides you with instructions on the preparation of a personal welfare lasting power of attorney (LPA). Based on these instructions you prepare the LPA and visit the client who is critically ill in hospital. The client agrees to the LPA.

Again, if the contract is made during the visit to your office then the Regulations probably do not apply. In order to establish whether the contract was made at your office, you would need to consider carefully the content of what was said in your office, and whether the relative had authority to enter into a contract on the client's behalf.

If the contract was made during the hospital visit then limb (a) of regulation 5 would not apply; the visit was not to the client's home or place or work or to the home of another individual. However, there would be a question as to whether limb (b) would apply. This depends on whether the hospital visit amounted to an 'excursion' organised by you away from your business premises.

As a matter of construction, this is not wholly clear. However, what you have done here is to make arrangements to travel to a place other than your business premises (ie the hospital), for the purpose of meeting a client or potential client.

This situation may fall within limb (b) of regulation 5. In the absence of any case-law on the question, it may be wise to treat the Regulations as applicable to any contract with the client that you make during the hospital visit.

Example 3

At the request of a client you visit the client's work place. During this visit a contractual agreement is made that you will undertake work for the client. The client has asked this work to be done urgently and provides you with a request in writing for work to commence before the 7 day cancellation period expires. You commence work but receive a cancellation notice from the client 6 days after the agreement is reached.

In this situation the Regulations apply to the contract: it falls within regulation 5(a). The client is entitled to cancel the contract, despite the written request. However, you are entitled to claim payment in accordance with the reasonable requirements of the contract for services that were supplied before the cancellation: regulation 9(2). If the client had not provided a written request to start work before the cancellation period expired, then the solicitor would not be entitled to payment: regulation 9(3). See section 5 below for discussion of regulation 9.

Example 4

A Solicitor organises for a client to accompany him/her to a trade conference and during this conference the consumer makes an offer for work to be done by the solicitor. The solicitor goes back to his/her business premises and then informs the client that the offer has been accepted.

The Regulations apply to this situation. The client's offer was made during an excursion falling within regulation 5(b). The contract was made following that offer, and so would fall within regulation 5(c).

If the offer was made at the home of one of the client's friends, then the offer would be made during a visit falling within regulation 5(a); hence, if the contract was made following that offer, again, it would fall within regulation 5(c).

---

4   ACTIONS REQUIRED WHERE THE REGULATIONS APPLY

If the Regulations apply then the client has a right to cancel the contract during the cancellation period (regulation 7(1)). The cancellation period is the period of 7 days starting with the date of receipt by the client of a notice of the right to cancel (regulation 2(1)).

4.1   Providing written notice

Under regulation 7(2) you must give the client a written notice of his right to cancel the contract. Notice must be given as follows:

- In the first and second situations described in section 3 above, notice must be given at the time the contract is made.
- In situation three (as detailed in limb (c) of regulation 5), the notice must be given at the time the offer is made by the client.

Regulations 7(3) and 7(5) set out what the notice must contain.

Regulation 7(4) stipulates that you must incorporate the notice in the contract where the contract is wholly or partly in writing.

If incorporated in the contract or another document the notice of the right to cancel must be set out in a separate box with the heading 'Notice of the Right to Cancel'. It must have as much prominence as any other information in the contract or document apart from the heading and the names of the parties to the contract and any information inserted in handwriting: see regulation 7(5).

Draft example templates have been provided in section 6 to assist in the preparation of a standardised notice.

4.2   Failure to provide notice

If you enter into a contract to which the Regulations apply, and you do not give the client a notice of the right to cancel and the information required by regulation 7, then you will not be able to enforce the contract against the client: see regulation 7(6).

For instance, you will not be able to sue under the contract for fees for work done. But the contract will not be void, and so it will still be enforceable against you by the client.

4.3   Current contracts

You may have entered into a contract to which these Regulations apply, since 1 October 2008, without advising your client of the right to cancel under the Regulations. If so and all fees remain outstanding in such a matter, you should consider advising the client of the right to cancel.

You may consider entering into a new agreement that meets the requirements, to ensure that you are entitled to payment of any fees or costs due for future work.

Even if you enter into a new contract, you may be unable to recover fees for work already done, if you ought to have given notice of the right to cancel but failed to do so.

This matter is not free of doubt and is likely to remain so until an opportunity presents itself for the court to provide further guidance. Until then, to minimise the risk of potential difficulties an alternative option may be to offer to vary the terms of the agreement where this is a possibility and is appropriate in the circumstances. However, when inviting the client to agree to any variation you must explain clearly what is proposed and the full implications of any agreement to vary the contract.

If you have entered into a conditional fee agreement (CFA) without giving notification of the right to cancel, then where applicable, you may consider entering into a retrospective CFA which provides notification of this right.

You must, however, fully explain to the client the reason for the new contract and the consequences of such an agreement.

With regard to CFAs, the courts do appear to have recognised that inviting a client to agree a retrospective CFA is an acceptable means of remedying certain failures to comply with the legislative requirements to provide prescribed information to clients prior to entering a CFA to which those requirements would apply. It therefore seems likely that entering a retrospective CFA with a client in order to comply with the Cancellation of Contracts Regulations is a realistic option to consider in respect of any client whose CFA came into existence after 1 October 2008 but without the requisite notice.

With regard to any amendments to CFAs you should ensure that you take into account the Civil Procedure Rules 1998 (Parts 43–45), and in particular the requirement under 44.15 to provide information regarding the existence of the CFA to the court and other parties to the litigation, and inform them within 7 days of any amendments that may lead to additional liabilities. Failure to do so may result in additional liabilities being irrecoverable.

5   CRIMINAL OFFENCES

It is a criminal offence to fail to provide written notice of the right to cancel the contract: regulation 17. The offence is one of strict liability and carries up to the maximum penalty for a summary offence.

The duty of enforcing regulation 17 is placed on weights and measures authorities (ie local trading standards departments): see regulation 21(1). They have various powers of investigation, including powers to require the production of documents: regulation 22. However, you cannot be required to produce a document which you would be entitled to refuse to produce in High Court litigation on grounds of legal professional privilege: regulation 22(6).

There are various offences in connection with obstructing, or failing to co-operate with, officers of enforcement authorities. On summary conviction these carry a fine not exceeding level 3 on the standard scale: see regulation 23.

6   THE COOLING-OFF PERIOD

The cancellation period lasts for 7 days, beginning with the date when the client receives notice of the right to cancel: see regulation 2(1).

During that period the client can cancel the contract by serving a written notice indicating that s/he wishes to cancel it. The notice does not have to be in any specific form.

If a client exercises their right to cancel, then s/he is not liable to pay for work done before the cancellation, unless s/he has made a written request for the performance of the contract to begin before the end of the cancellation period: regulation 9(1)–(3).

6.1   Receiving notice

Notice of cancellation can be given by email (see regulation 8(6)), and you must inform clients of this fact in your written notification of your right to cancel.

In practical terms this means that you must be able to deal with notices sent by email, even if you do not usually conduct correspondence by email or accept service of documents by this means.

A cancellation notice sent by email is taken to have been served on the day on which it is sent: regulation 8(6). It is unclear whether an email notice that is not actually received by you is an effective notice of cancellation under the Regulations.

A cancellation notice sent by post is taken to have been served at the time of posting, whether or not it is actually received: regulation 8(5).

There is some risk that a client will serve an effective notice of cancellation, without you becoming aware that this has been done. To avoid this situation you may wish to check with clients, shortly after the end of the cancellation period, that they have not exercised their right to cancel.

6.2   Dealing with urgent requests

If your client wishes you to do work urgently, your client can request in writing that you commence work before the cancellation period expires. This request means the client must pay for services provided such as the instructions, even if the contract is later cancelled. This request does not mean that the client has waived the right to cancel the contract within the cancellation period.

Absent such a written request, you are not legally obliged to start work on performing the contract before the end of the cancellation period: regulation 9(3)(a). However, see also section 6.3 below.

6.3   Vulnerable clients

You must ensure that the client fully understands the nature, effect, benefits, risks and foreseeable consequences of requesting work to commence before the cancellation period expires, in order to enable them to form a view as to the wisdom of the proposed transaction.

Assessing your client's understanding of the implications of commencing work straight away may help you to determine whether they have the capacity to make the decision, or whether they are subject to undue influence from family, beneficiaries or others.

Where you are requested to attend a weak or seriously ill client it may be impracticable or inappropriate either to obtain a written request, or to wait for the cancellation period to expire before you start work.

These situations are very difficult. You will need to balance your interest in securing payment for work done, with your professional duty to act in the best interests of the client.

6.4   Payment taken before the cooling-off period expires

Unless there is a request to commence work before the cooling-off period expires, any payment taken before the end of the cooling off period will be repayable under regulation 10 should the client cancel the contract under regulation 8.

7   TEMPLATES: PROVIDING WRITTEN NOTICE

Template 1: contracts made in homes or workplaces or during excursions

Suggested template for written Notice of right to cancel, for use in cases falling within regulation 5(a) or (b) of the Cancellation of Contracts made in a Consumer's Home or Place of Work etc Regulations 2008 ('the Regulations').

Notice of the right to cancel

This Notice has been provided to you because you have entered into a contract to which the Cancellation of Contracts made in a Consumer's Home or Place of Work Regulations 2008 ('the Regulations') apply. The contract is for the supply to you of goods or services. The person providing the goods or services is referred to in the Regulations as 'the trader'.

Under the Regulations, you have the right to cancel this contract if you wish to do so. This Notice explains how to exercise this right. It also gives you other information that is required by the Regulations.

In order to exercise your right to cancel the contract, you need to deliver or send a cancellation notice, that is, a written notice that you wish to cancel the contract. You can use the cancellation form provided below if you wish, but you do not have to do so. You can send your notification by email if you prefer.

Any cancellation notice should be delivered or sent to [name of person] at [postal address] or at [email address].

You have 7 days in which to serve a cancellation notice. The period of 7 days begins with the date when you receive this Notice. This 7 day period is referred to in the Regulations as 'the cancellation period'.

Under the Regulations, a cancellation notice is treated as being served as soon as it is sent or posted to the trader. A cancellation notice sent by electronic communication is treated as being served from the day when it is sent to the trader.

If you agree in writing that the performance of this contract should begin before the end of the cancellation period, then even if you cancel the contract you may still be required to pay for goods or services supplied before the cancellation.

If you enter into a related credit agreement, then that agreement will be automatically cancelled if the contract is cancelled. A 'related credit agreement' means an agreement under which fixed sum credit which fully or partly covers the price under the contract is granted to you by the trader, or by another person under an arrangement made between that person and the trader.

The identity of the trader providing goods or services under this contract is [insert name of solicitor or firm that is party to the contract, including any trading name]

The reference number, code or other details to enable the contract to be identified is [insert details]

This Notice is dated [insert date when the Notice is given to the client]

[You must include with the written Notice a cancellation form as a detachable slip, in accordance with the form set out in Schedule 4 Part II to the Regulations. Schedule 4 Part II is reproduced at Template 3 below. You must complete the cancellation form in accordance with the notes in Schedule 4 Part II, before you give the written notice to the client.]

Notes on the use of the above template

- The Template is designed to meet the requirement that, where a contract between you and your client falls within the Regulations, you must give your client written notice of their right to cancel under the Regulations. Regulation 7, and Schedule 4, set out strict requirements as to the form of the notice. You are strongly advised to read the Regulations yourself in their entirety in order to understand the duties that they impose. Remember that failure to give a written notice complying with the requirements of regulation 7 and Schedule 4 is a criminal offence.
- The above Template is designed to be used in cases falling within regulation 5(a) or (b) of the Regulations. In these cases, written notice of the right to terminate must be given to the client at the time when the contract is made. There is a separate Template for cases falling within regulation 5(c): see Template 2.
- Note that the written notice must include a cancellation form. This must be in the form set out in Schedule 4 Part II to the Regulations, reproduced at Template 3 below.
- Note that where the contract is wholly or partly in writing the notice of the right to cancel must be incorporated in the same document: regulation 7(4).
- Note that if incorporated in the contract or another document the Notice of the right to cancel must be set out in a separate box with the heading 'Notice of the Right to Cancel'; and
- have as much prominence as any other information in the contract or document apart from the heading and the names of the parties to the contract and any information inserted in handwriting. See regulation 7(5).

Template 2: contracts made after a visit or excursion

Suggested template for written Notice of right to cancel, for use in cases falling within regulation 5(c) of the Cancellation of Contracts made in a Consumer's Home or Place of Work etc Regulations 2008 ('the Regulations').

Notice of the right to cancel

This Notice has been provided to you because you have offered to enter into a contract to which the Cancellation of Contracts made in a Consumer's Home or Place of Work Regulations 2008 ('the Regulations') would apply. The contract would be for the supply to you of goods or services. The person who would provide the goods or services is referred to in the Regulations as 'the trader'.

Under the Regulations, you have the right to cancel this contract if you wish to do so. This Notice explains how to exercise this right. It also gives you other information that is required by the Regulations.

In order to exercise your right to cancel the contract, you need to deliver or send a cancellation notice, that is, a written notice that you wish to cancel the contract. You can use the cancellation form provided below if you wish, but you do not have to do so. You can send your notification by email if you prefer.

Any cancellation notice should be delivered or sent to [name of person] at [postal address] or at [email address]

You have 7 days in which to serve a cancellation notice. The period of 7 days begins with the date when you receive this Notice. This 7 day period is referred to in the Regulations as 'the cancellation period'.

Under the Regulations, a cancellation notice is treated as being served as soon as it is sent or posted to the trader. A cancellation notice sent by electronic communication is treated as being served from the day when it is sent to the trader.

If you agree in writing that the performance of this contract should begin before the end of the cancellation period, then even if you cancel the contract you may still be required to pay for goods or services supplied before the cancellation.

If you enter into a related credit agreement, then that agreement will be automatically cancelled if the contract is cancelled. A 'related credit agreement' means an agreement under which fixed sum credit which fully or partly covers the price under the contract is granted to you by the trader, or by another person under an arrangement made between that person and the trader.

The identity of the trader providing goods or services under this contract is [insert name of solicitor or firm that is party to the contract, including any trading name]

The reference number, code or other details to enable the contract to be identified is [insert details]

This Notice is dated [insert date when the Notice is given to the client]

[You must include with the written Notice a cancellation form as a detachable slip, in accordance with the form set out in Schedule 4 Part II to the Regulations. Schedule 4 Part II is reproduced at Template 3 below. You must complete the cancellation form in accordance with the notes in Schedule 4 Part II, before you give the written notice to the client.]

Notes on the use of the above template

- The Template is designed to meet the requirement that, where a contract between you and your client falls within the Regulations, you must give your client written notice of their right to cancel under the Regulations. Regulation 7, and Schedule 4, set out strict requirements as to the form of the notice. You are strongly advised to read the Regulations yourself in their entirety in order to understand the duties that they impose. Remember that failure to give a written notice complying with the requirements of regulation 7 and Schedule 4 is a criminal offence.
- The above Template is designed to be used in cases falling within regulation 5(c) of the Regulations. In these cases, written notice of the right to terminate must be given to the client at the time when the client makes an offer falling within regulation 5(c). There is a separate Template for cases falling within regulation 5(a) or (b): see Template 1.
- Note that the written notice must include a cancellation form. This must be in the form set out in Schedule 4 Part II to the Regulations, reproduced at Template 3 below.
- Note that where the contract is wholly or partly in writing the notice of the right to cancel must be incorporated in the same document: regulation 7(4).
- Note that if incorporated in the contract or another document the Notice of the right to cancel must be set out in a separate box with the heading 'Notice of the Right to Cancel'; and
- have as much prominence as any other information in the contract or document apart from the heading and the names of the parties to the contract and any information inserted in handwriting. See regulation 7(5).

Template 3: Schedule IV Part II to the Cancellation of Contracts made in a Consumer's Home or Place of Work etc Regulations 2008

If you wish to cancel the contract you MUST DO SO IN WRITING and deliver personally or send (which may be by electronic mail) this to the person named below. You may use this form if you want to but you do not have to.

(Complete, detach and return this form ONLY IF YOU WISH TO CANCEL THE CONTRACT.)

To: .... [trader to insert name and address of person to whom notice may be given.]

I/We (delete as appropriate) hereby give notice that I/we (delete as appropriate) wish to cancel my/our (delete as appropriate) contract .... [trader to insert reference number, code or other details to enable the contract or offer to be identified. He may also insert the name and address of the consumer.]

Signed

Name and Address

Date

8   MORE INFORMATION

8.1   Legal and other requirements

- Consumer Protection (Cancellation of Contracts made in a Consumer's Home or Place of Work etc) Regulations 2008
- Civil Procedure Rules 1998

8.2   Further products and support

8.2.1   *Department for Business Enterprise and Regulatory Reform*

The Department has provided explanatory notes on the regulation.

8.2.2   *Practice Advice Line*

The Law Society provides support for solicitors on a wide range of areas of practice. Practice Advice can be contacted on 0870 606 2522 from 09:00 to 17:00 on weekdays.

8.2.3   *Solicitors Regulation Authority Contact Centre*

Assists solicitors with enquiries relating to practising certificates, continuing professional development (CPD) and other general enquiries.

- Telephone 0870 606 2555
- Visit the Solicitors Regulation Authority website [**www.sra.org.uk**]

8.2.4   Law Society publications

Drafting Commercial Agreements

**[http://bookshop.lawsociety.org.uk/ecom_lawsoc/public/
saleproduct.jsf?catalogueCode=9781853286049]**

8.2.5   Training and events

Private Companies after the Companies Act 2011

**[http://cpdcentre.lawsociety.org.uk/course/1261/private-companies-after-the-
companies-act-2006]**

Disputed wills practice note

6 October 2011

1 INTRODUCTION

1.1 Who should read this practice note?

Solicitors dealing with wills and probate.

1.2 What is the issue?

If a will you have prepared is disputed you may be asked to disclose information about the circumstances surrounding its preparation and execution.

Law Society advice on this issue was affirmed by the Court of Appeal in *Larke* v *Nugus* SW vol123 (1979) CA p337 and later reported in (2000) WTLR 1033. This practice note highlights that advice and provides supplementary information on disclosing such information, the consequences of failing to do so, and protecting the estate.

1.3 Professional conduct

The following section of the SRA Code is relevant to this issue:

• Chapter 4 on Confidentiality and disclosure

1.4 Status of this practice note

Practice notes are issued by the Law Society for the use and benefit of its members. They represent the Law Society's view of good practice in a particular area. They are not intended to be the only standard of good practice that solicitors can follow. You are not required to follow them, but doing so will make it easier to account to oversight bodies for your actions.

Practice notes are not legal advice, nor do they necessarily provide a defence to complaints of misconduct or of inadequate professional service. While care has been taken to ensure that they are accurate, up to date and useful, the Law Society will not accept any legal liability in relation to them.

For queries or comments on this practice note, contact the Law Society's Practice Advice Service.

1.5 Terminology

Must – A specific requirement in legislation or of a principle, rule, outcome or other mandatory provision in the SRA Handbook. You must comply, unless there are specific exemptions or defences provided for in relevant legislation or the SRA Handbook.

Should–

- Outside of a regulatory context, good practice for most situations in the Law Society's view. In the case of the SRA Handbook, an indicative behaviour or other non-mandatory provision (such as may be set out in notes or guidance).
- These may not be the only means of complying with legislative or regulatory requirements and there may be situations where the suggested route is not the best possible route to meet the needs of your client. However, if you do not follow the suggested route, you should be able to justify to oversight bodies why the alternative approach you have taken is appropriate, either for your practice, or in the particular retainer.

May – A non-exhaustive list of options for meeting your obligations or running your practice. Which option you choose is determined by the profile of the individual practice, client or retainer. You may be required to justify why this was an appropriate option to oversight bodies.

SRA Code – SRA Code of Conduct 2011

SRA – Solicitors Regulation Authority

Testator – The person who made the will

Executor – The person responsible for carrying out the terms of the will

Beneficiary – The person/s named in the will

Fiduciary – The person entrusted with property or power on behalf of the beneficiary

Subpoena – The summoning of a witness or the submission of evidence to the court

Grant ad colligenda bona defuncti – The application for a temporary grant from the Probate Registry to deal with the assets of a deceased estate

2 SRA PRINCIPLES

There are ten mandatory principles which apply to all those the SRA regulates and to all aspects of practice. The principles can be found in the SRA Handbook.

The principles apply to solicitors or managers of authorised bodies who are practising from an office outside the UK. They also apply if you are a lawyer-controlled body practising from an office outside the UK.

3 CIRCUMSTANCES IN WHICH YOU SHOULD DISCLOSE THE CONTENTS OF A WILL

Under the SRA Code, Chapter 4 on Confidentiality and disclosure, your duty of confidentiality continues after the end of the retainer. When the client dies, the right to confidentiality passes to the personal representatives; an administrator's authority does not begin until the court grants letters of administration.

3.1 Legal background

The question of confidentiality in relation to a disputed will was considered in *Larke* v *Nugus*. At that time the Law Society's advice on disputed wills was:

If the testator is dead, the solicitor must not disclose any information before probate is granted, except to the executors, without the consent of the executors. But this will not necessarily apply where a solicitor is asked to disclose information about a will which he has prepared and which is in dispute.

Privilege cannot be claimed by one person claiming under a deceased testator's will as against another person having a similar claim in respect of matters communicated by the deceased to the solicitor during the lifetime of the deceased. The testator's solicitor could be compelled by the court under subpoena to answer questions directed to eliciting communications made to him by the testator in the course of preparing the will if put to him or her by either party.

Where a serious dispute arises as to the validity of a will, beyond the mere entering of a caveat and the solicitor's knowledge makes him or her a material witness, then the solicitor should make available a statement of his evidence regarding the execution of the will and the circumstances surrounding it to anyone concerned in the proving or challenging of that will, whether or not the solicitor acted for those who were propounding the will.

This advice was confirmed and upheld in the case by the Court of Appeal (Civil Division) in *Larke v Nugus.*

The Court of Appeal made it clear that the information required related to both:

- the circumstances in which the testator gave instructions for the will
- the circumstances in which the will was executed

3.2   Senior Courts Act 1981

If you have prepared a will you have knowledge that makes you a material witness if the will is disputed. The court has power under the Senior Courts Act 1981, s122, to order persons with knowledge of any document that is or purports to be a testamentary document to attend court and answer questions relating to the document.

You should therefore provide the information in advance to try to limit the costs of a full hearing.

3.3   Civil Procedure Rules

The court has power under Rule 31.16 of the Civil Procedure Rules to order pre-action disclosure of documents in order to either:

- dispose fairly of the anticipated proceedings; or
- assist the dispute to be resolved without proceedings; or save costs

You should make available any documents in your possession that are relevant to the proceedings to avoid the cost of unnecessary applications to court. Providing this information promptly when a will is initially challenged may dispel suspicions and save costs in the long run.

You should make a full attendance note at the time the will is prepared. You should also preserve the file. See Law Society Practice Note on Retention of Files.

4   GOOD PRACTICE ON RECEIPT OF A REQUEST FOR INFORMATION

4.1   Where there is no suggestion of negligence

The following applies where a will you have prepared is in dispute, but there is no suggestion of professional negligence.

When requested, in what is known as a '*Larke* v *Nugus* letter', you should provide a full statement of evidence as to the preparation of the will, and the circumstances in which it was executed to anyone who has an interest in the dispute, whether or not you are acting for any of the parties:

You should also, with the consent of any third party personal representatives, make available a copy of requested documents.

The quickest and easiest way of complying with such requests will often be to copy the contents of the will file.

As a potential witness in proceedings, you may not charge for time spent compiling the statement or documents however a reasonable charge may be made for photocopying.

4.2   Where there is a possibility of negligence

You should take the following steps where there is a possibility of negligence in the preparation of the will:

1. inform any lay executors and beneficiaries of the will that they may wish to take independent advice as to whether or not the will was negligently drafted, and
2. immediately inform your practice's insurers of the existence of a potential claim

5   CONSEQUENCES OF FAILURE TO PROVIDE FULL INFORMATION

In *Larke* v *Nugus*, the Court of Appeal refused to order those challenging the will to pay the costs of the challenge even though the will was found to be valid. This was because the solicitor who had prepared the will refused to make information available at an early stage which, had it been given, could have prevented a full trial. The claimants' costs, therefore, were ordered to be paid from the estate and reduced the amount available for the beneficiaries of the valid will.

The beneficiaries of an estate that has been reduced in this way would be justified in bringing an action against the solicitor who had failed to disclose the information at an early stage to recover the lost costs.

As the purpose of a *Larke* v *Nugus* letter is to prevent money being spent on futile litigation by the provision of early pre-action disclosure, the onus is on you to provide a prompt reply and relevant evidence to facilitate early settlement.

Providing a response shortly before trial, when most of the costs have been incurred, is unlikely to protect you from an adverse costs order. You should therefore provide a full response to a request within a reasonable period, for example: two to three weeks, or as long as it is necessary to:

- retrieve the file
- consider the contents
- copy any necessary parts of the file
- provide the statement to the relevant parties.

6   RISKS OF ACTING IN DISPUTES

You may find yourself in a difficult position, if a will you prepared is disputed, particularly if the will appoints you as executor. You may feel strongly that the will is valid and that those disputing it are misguided but you should consider your position carefully.

6.1 Risk of incurring costs

As an executor you are a fiduciary with duties to the beneficiaries of the estate, whoever they turn out to be. If you are partisan in the litigation, you risk a costs order being made against you personally. Provided you act neutrally in any litigation the costs of the executor should come out of the estate. So far as the warring parties are concerned, it is no longer the case that costs in probate litigation will necessarily be ordered from the estate. Costs are at the discretion of the court, and it is increasingly the case that the unsuccessful party will have to bear them.

To avoid being at risk of costs you should therefore remain neutral and allow the beneficiaries of the will or next of kin to pursue the litigation. Your only obligation in the proceedings is to provide information and to preserve the estate.

6.2 Conducting litigation on behalf of the beneficiary

There may sometimes be circumstances in which it is difficult for the beneficiaries to conduct the litigation and you, as executor, may wish to do so on their behalf. If so you should:

- be clear that you are making yourself a party to the litigation with all the risks of adverse costs orders being made against you
- protect yourself where possible by taking out an indemnity for costs from adult beneficiaries

The safest course of action is for you to suggest to the beneficiaries that they seek separate advice.

7 PROTECTING THE ESTATE PENDING RESOLUTION OF THE DISPUTE

7.1 Application for temporary grant

Irrespective of whether or not a particular will is valid, steps should be taken in relation to the assets and liabilities of an estate. These can include the duty of the executors to ensure that assets must be secured and liabilities paid. However, the identity of the true executors may be uncertain if the will is in dispute. In these circumstances, the parties to the dispute, and those advising them, should consider at an early stage how best to protect the estate.

Where it is possible, after the agreement of the parties to the dispute, you or another agreed party, usually a professional, should apply to the Probate Registry for a temporary grant, or grant ad colligenda bona defuncti, to deal with the assets and protect them until a full grant can be obtained.

7.2 Agreement regarding steps in the administration

Where an executor or administrator has already taken a grant, you should agree with the parties to the litigation what steps will be taken in the administration. It is easy for an executor who is involved in a dispute to overlook simple steps such as cashing in premium bonds after they cease to be eligible for prizes or investing cash in high interest accounts.

8 MORE INFORMATION

8.1 Legal and other requirements

- Senior Courts Act 1981, s 122
- Civil Procedure Rules, Rule 31.16

8.2   Further products and support

8.2.1   *Law Society Practice Advice Service*

The Law Society provides support for solicitors on a wide range of areas of practice. Practice Advice can be contacted on 0870 606 2522 from 09.00 to 17.00 on weekdays.

8.2.2   *Professional Ethics Helpline*

Solicitors Regulation Authority's Professional Ethics Helpline for advice on conduct issues.

[www.sra.org.uk/contactus.page]

8.2.3   *Practice notes*

* File retention: trusts
* File retention: wills and probate

8.2.4   *Law Society products and publications*

* *Probate Practitioner's Handbook*, 6th edition
* *Will Draftsman Handbook*, 8th edition
* Inheritance Act Claims
* Law Society membership benefit: Certainty

8.2.5   *Training and events*

* CPD course: Private Client Update: Current Hot Topics and Lessons to be Learnt

    [http://cpdcentre.lawsociety.org.uk/course/1948/private-client-update-current-hot-topics-and-lessons-to-be-learnt]
* CPD course: Elderly Client Update

    [http://cpdcentre.lawsociety.org.uk/course/1947/elderly-client-update]
* CPD course: Gazette CPD – January 2011

    [http://cpdcentre.lawsociety.org.uk/course/1220/gazette-cpd-january-2011]

8.2.6   *Association of Contentious Trust and Probate Practitioners*

The Association provides resources for solicitors, barristers and legal executives working in this area, including a letter template for requesting information from solicitors about the preparation of wills.
   Visit the ACTAPS website [**http://actaps.com**].

8.3   Acknowledgements

The Law Society thanks the Wills and Equity Committee for their assistance with this practice note.

Estate administration: banking protocols practice note

28 January 2013

This practice note is relevant to any solicitor involved in the administration of estates.

Solicitors often experience difficulty and delay during the estate administration process in relation to assets held by banks and building societies.

This practice note contains protocols that set out procedures agreed with banks and building societies to clarify and speed up the estate administration process. This is a joint initiative with the Society of Trust and Estate Practitioners (STEP) and the British Bankers' Association (BBA).

The following protocols have been agreed. The uniform protocol covers all major banks (including Lloyds and HSBC). A separate protocol for Nationwide is provided below.

Note that these do not address professional conduct or legal requirements.

FURTHER HELP

Practice Advice Service

The Practice Advice Service is a dedicated support line for members of the Law Society, which is able to help solicitors with a wide range of practice and procedure issues. The service is staffed by experienced solicitors with access to a wide range of information sources. The Practice Advice Service can be contacted on 0870 606 2522 from 09:00 to 17:00 on weekdays.

More information on the Practice Advice Service.

Solicitors Regulation Authority

The Solicitors Regulation Authority regulates solicitors in England and Wales. It makes and enforces the SRA Code of Conduct 2011.

BANKING PRACTICES PROTOCOL – ESTATE ADMINISTRATION

This protocol has been agreed between the British Bankers' Association, the Law Society of England and Wales and the Society of Trust and Estate Practitioners. The purpose is to bring clarity to probate-related dealings between advisors and banks. It covers the handling of current, savings, credit card and unsecured loan accounts but does not necessarily apply to investment, pensions or insurance matters, or to accounts held by associated companies or businesses.

Set out below is the information that the banks will normally require from the solicitor/ STEP member on first contact or shortly afterwards. If this information is provided, delays in dealing with accounts or investments will be reduced.

1. Sight of an official copy of the Register (ie death certificate) issued by the General Register Office or the solicitor's death certificate verification form. Where a death certificate has not been issued as an inquest is required some banks will accept an interim certificate issued by the coroner.

2. Date of death.

3. List of deceased's names in which accounts were or may have been held, and the last address of the deceased prior to death or admission to hospital/nursing home etc. Also the date of birth of the deceased.

4. Account numbers and sort codes of relevant accounts where these are known.

5. Verification of the status of the solicitor/probate practitioner to include confirmation of authority to act on behalf of executors (where the deceased left a will) or next of kin (where deceased left no will). In the case of solicitors a letter on headed paper with the Solicitors Regulation Authority registration number quoted should ensure that delay is kept to a minimum. The verification procedure for STEP members who are not solicitors to be agreed direct between STEP and the individual bank. Confirmation that the enquirer is a STEP member can be obtained by reference to that member's inclusion on the STEP website – **www.step.org**

6. Correct address for correspondence in connection with the accounts of the deceased.

7. Approximate value of the estate where available.

8. Information confirming the existence of the will and the names of executors. Banks may require sight of the original will or a solicitor certified copy of the will. Set out below is the information that the solicitor/STEP member is likely to require from the bank and also an outline of how the bank might normally respond to such requests. (Some banks may require the consent of the surviving account holder before releasing information on joint accounts.)

Set out below is the information that the solicitor/STEP member is likely to require from the bank and also an outline of how the bank might normally respond to such requests. (Some banks may require the consent of the surviving account holder before releasing information on joint accounts.)

9. Confirmation of the numbers of all accounts in the name of the deceased, including those held jointly, subject to the solicitor/STEP member providing the full name and address of the deceased. It is the practice of some banks to require the consent of the surviving account holder before releasing information on joint accounts.

10. Details of the balances on all accounts (including joint accounts) at the date of death and, where appropriate, the amount of accrued interest to the date of death. Movements on all accounts between the date of death and the date of the bank providing account information where this is specifically requested. It is the practice of some banks to require the consent of the surviving account holder before releasing information on joint accounts.

11. Where a specific request is made, the bank would place current account balances on deposit, and confirm that this has been done, pending closure on production of the grant of representation. Individual banks may wish to invoke particular procedures in regard to this provision.

12. The provision of access to the solicitor/STEP member or an agreed agent to inspect and value any items that the bank is holding in safe custody on behalf of the deceased.

13. Where a specific request is made, provision of a certificate showing any interest paid and tax deducted during the period from 6 April last to the date of death (and for the previous tax year).

14. Where a specific request is made, details of all standing orders and direct debits in force at the date of death and confirmation that a stop has been placed on them where they

relate to an account in the sole name of the deceased. Where the account is in joint names, the instructions of the survivor will be required to cancel any standing orders or direct debits.

15. Where a specific request is made, confirmation that the bank will allow the balance on accounts to be used before production of the grant of representation for payment of inheritance tax and the funeral bill. The bank may also allow these funds to be used for the payment of probate fees. The bank may require copies of relevant documentation, in accordance with the individual bank's procedures. Irrespective of the purpose of a release of balances the bank may require an indemnity or possibly a solicitor's undertaking. In all cases this confirmation is subject to the exercise of the bank's right of set-off to the extent permitted by law where there are also debts due to the bank.

16. Confirmation that the correct address for correspondence has been noted on all accounts in the name of the deceased. When requested correspondence should be sent to the solicitor/STEP member acting for the deceased's legal representative. It is the practice of some banks to require the authority of the executor or next of kin before doing this.

17. The bank will aim to respond to the requests made under paragraphs 9–16 above within 15 working days.

Account Closure

18. On closing an account, the bank to confirm that the account has been closed; the closing balance will be sent within a reasonable time.

19. Closing bank statements and the closing balance to be sent to the solicitor/STEP member acting for the deceased's legal representative unless the legal representative advises the bank otherwise. Where a specific request is made bank statements from the date of death to closure will be provided. A fee may be payable for the provision of bank statements from the date of death to closure.

20. When a deceased holds both credit and debit balances with the bank, the bank will apply set-off rules to the extent permitted by law, providing the solicitor/STEP member with settlement on the net figure. The solicitor/STEP member will be advised of the net figure by letter or an assets and liabilities pro forma. The types of accounts covered in calculating a net balance will include: savings accounts, current accounts, unsecured loan accounts and credit card accounts.

21. The time periods suggested in relation to account closures are:

    a.) Closing balance to be sent no more than ten working days after receipt of grant of representation (either the original or official copy required) and the legal repre-sentatives' signed closure instructions – the period could be longer for accounts other than current and normal savings accounts or in circumstances where safe custody assets have not been collected.

    b.) Closing balance statement to be sent no more than the ten working days from closure of the account.

22. Without a grant of representation the bank may, at its discretion, require a signed indemnity form if it is prepared to release balances in the deceased's bank accounts.

BANKING PRACTICES PROTOCOL BETWEEN NATIONWIDE BUILDING SOCIETY, THE LAW SOCIETY OF ENGLAND AND WALES AND THE SOCIETY OF TRUST AND ESTATE PRACTITIONERS

This protocol has been agreed between Nationwide Building Society, the Law Society of England and Wales and the Society of Trust and Estate Practitioners. The purpose is to bring clarity to probate-related dealings between advisers and Nationwide Building Society.

Set out below is the information Nationwide Building Society will require from the solicitor/STEP member on first contact or shortly afterwards. If this information is provided, delays in dealing with the account or investments will be reduced.

What information will Nationwide Building Society require from the solicitor/probate practitioner on a first approach?

1. Death certificate/death certificate verification form/Interim death certificate.
2. Date of death.
3. List of names, such as maiden names, in which accounts were held.
4. Verification of the status of the practitioner to include confirmation of authority to act on behalf of the executors/next of kin. In the case of solicitors a letter on headed paper with the Law Society roll number quoted; and in the case of STEP members a letter on headed paper with the STEP membership number quoted will be sufficient.
5. Correct address for correspondence in connection with the accounts of the deceased.
6. Approximate value of the estate.
7. Information regarding the will to confirm the existence of the will and the names of the executors.

Set out below is the information that the solicitor/STEP member is likely to require from Nationwide Building Society and also an outline of how Nationwide Building Society might respond to such requests.

1. Confirmation of the numbers of all accounts in the name of the deceased (including those held jointly).
2. Details of the balance on all accounts in the deceased's name (including joint accounts) at the date of death and, where appropriate, the amount of accrued interest to the date of death.
3. A certificate showing any interest paid and tax deducted during the period from 6 April last to the date of death [and for the previous tax year].
4. Details of all standing orders and direct debits in force at the date of death and confirmation that a stop has been placed on them (Only applicable for sole accounts).
5. Confirmation that the Nationwide Building Society will allow the balance on accounts to be used before production of the grant of probate for payment of inheritance tax, settlement of funeral expenses and payment of probate fees.
6. Correct address for correspondence in connection with the accounts of the deceased.

Account closure

1. Information sent no more than fifteen working days after receipt of the request.
2. Closing balance sent no more than ten working days after receipt of grant of probate.
3. Closing balance statement sent no more than ten working days from closure of the account.
4. When a deceased customer holds both credit and debit balances on accounts with the Nationwide Building Society, Nationwide will apply set-off rules, and clear any Nationwide debts, providing the solicitor/STEP member with settlement on the net figure. The solicitor will be advised of the net balance via the date of death figures.

File retention: wills and probate practice note

6 October 2011

1 INTRODUCTION

1.1 Who should read this practice note?

Managing partners, probate and trust practitioners and other practice staff involved in the retention, archiving and storage of original wills and files relating to the preparation of wills, lifetime gifts and estate administration.

1.2 What are the issues?

It is essential that firms have a clear policy on the storage and destruction of the original files and documents.

With increasing longevity and diversity in relationships there are more disputes arising after death, as well as claims in respect of lifetime gifts.

Challenges to wills (especially if there are unequal gifts to children) or previous lifetime gifts or disposals of property at an undervalue often arise many years after the original advice was given.

You should keep records with the will which explain that appropriate advice was given to the client at the time of making the will. Without adequate records you or your firm may not be able to defend its position.

It is also essential to know who owns the various original documents and papers, especially after the death of your client.

1.3 Professional conduct

The following sections of the SRA Code are relevant to this issue:

- Chapter 1 on Client care
- Chapter 4 on Confidentiality and disclosure

1.4 Status of this practice note

Practice Notes are issued by the Law Society as a professional body for the benefit of its members. They represent the Law Society's view of good practice in a particular area. They are not intended to be the only standard, nor do they necessarily provide a defence to complaints of misconduct or of inadequate professional service. Solicitors are not required to follow them.

They do not constitute legal advice and, while care has been taken to ensure that they are accurate, up-to-date and useful, the Law Society will not accept any legal liability in relation to them.

For queries or comments on this practice note contact the Law Society's Practice Advice Service.

1.5   Terminology in this practice note

Must – a specific requirement in the Solicitors' Code of Conduct or legislation. You must comply, unless there are specific exemptions or defences provided for in the code of conduct or relevant legislation.

Should – good practice for most situations. If you deviate from this, you must be able to justify why this is appropriate, either for your firm, or in the particular retainer.

May – a non-exhaustive list of options for meeting your obligations. Which option you choose is determined by the risk profile of the individual firm, client or retainer. You must be able to justify why this was an appropriate option to oversight bodies.

2   SRA PRINCIPLES

There are ten mandatory principles which apply to all those the SRA regulates and to all aspects of practice. The principles can be found in the SRA Handbook.

When thinking about how to meet the outcomes in chapters 1 and 4 in the Code/Handbook, you must consider the principles which apply across the Handbook including the Code. You should always bear in mind what the ten principles are and use them as your starting point when implementing the outcomes.

3   WHO OWNS THE FILE?

An original will stored by you is the property of the client and after the client's death, it is the property of the estate.

The file also belongs to the client, subject to a limited number of documents which can be removed and belong to the firm.

Documents which come into existence during the retainer fall into four broad categories:

1. documents prepared by you for the client and which have been paid for by the client belong to the client;
2. documents prepared for the firm's own benefit or protection for which the client has not been charged belong to the firm;
3. documents and letters written by the client to you where property passes to you on despatch belong to the firm;
4. documents prepared by a third party during the course of the retainer and paid for by the client belong to the client (see *Cordery on Solicitors* for more details).

4   HOW LONG SHOULD FILES BE KEPT?

4.1   Retaining original wills

You should store the original will until after the death of the client, or until you are able to return the original to the client.

Some firms keep wills indefinitely, while others have a policy of holding the original will for fifty years from the date of its creation. There is no absolute rule, but you should always err on the side of caution, even if you believe or know that a later will has been made.

Your retainer should confirm what will happen to the original will and other supporting documentation that is not your property.

See 4.2 Destroying original wills and 4.3 Supporting documentation.

4.1.1   If the will is revoked

Even if a will is revoked you should keep a copy in your records.

It is possible that in cases where a will is challenged, undue influence is alleged or where an Inheritance (Provision for Family and Dependants) Act 1975 claim is made an earlier revoked will may be produced as evidence of a settled or disturbed pattern of behaviour or thought by the testator.

See 8.1.2 Legislation for further details.

4.2   Destroying original wills

You should not destroy an original will until any risk of a claim has passed.

See 6. Limitation periods for further details.

4.2.1   If the will is revoked

Before destruction of any original will you must consult the client. You should inform them that occasionally the validity of a subsequent will or wills might be challenged and then a prior will might be proved as the last will of the deceased.

As the limitation period does not start to run until the testator has died (see 6. Limitation periods), the general rules on limitations are of little relevance in this situation.

4.3   Retaining supporting documentation

Your retainer should confirm what will happen to the file. If your retainer is silent, you should contact your client and return any papers that you do not intend to retain.

There are three options you should consider:

- storing the file and any other supporting documentation for as long as the will is stored;
- reviewing the file and supporting documents so that the most important material is kept;
- keeping an abstract with the original will setting out significant matters.

If you decide to review the file, you will have to decide whether to review soon after the file is closed, or several years thereafter when the file destruction is imminent.

Reviewing the file soon after the end of the transaction is beneficial as relevant issues will be easier to recall.

If the file is left to be reviewed at a later stage bear in mind that relevant information may have been forgotten, or that you may no longer be working at the firm leaving the review to be carried out by someone unfamiliar with the matter.

4.3.1   Evidence of identity

The Money Laundering Regulations 2007 require that for 'relevant business', evidence of identity is to be retained for at least five years after the business relationship ends and for details of a transaction to be kept for a five year period from the date on which all activities taking place in the course of the transaction were completed.

The making of wills is not relevant business although trust and probate work is relevant business for the purposes of the Money Laundering Regulations 2007.

For further information see the Law Society's anti-money laundering practice note.

See 8.1.1 Practice notes.

4.3.2   Documents relating to VAT liability

The requirement under schedule 11, paragraph 6(3) of the Value Added Tax Act 1994 should also be taken into account. This says that records and papers relevant to VAT liability have to be kept for six years.

See 8.1.2 Legislation for details.

4.3.3   Documents recording contact with the client

You may also wish to keep a general file which records contact with a client and is not related to any major transaction, but contains all pertinent information about, for example, family dynamics or the intentions of the client.

You should not overlook such files when assessing what should be retained with the will. This general file should also contain meaningful abstracts of all relevant documents and major decisions.

4.3.4   Documents recording contact with the client

You should always keep a proper note of the advice that was given to the client together with details of the execution of the will/transfer if you were involved, regardless of whether or not you believe that there may be a subsequent challenge.

Even in situations where you have a good relationship with a number of members of a family, you should consider that you may not have the complete picture of family dynamics and finances.

Where there is an unusual disposal, such as a gift at an undervalue, or where the will leaves unequal shares to children, you should keep detailed records of the instructions and your advice.

See 4.5 Documents relating to lifetime gifts or transfers of property at an undervalue.

You should consider issues of conflict not just when the instructions are given, but if accepted how those instructions might be perceived subsequently.

4.4   Destroying supporting documentation

Any supporting documentation that is not your property should not be destroyed without written permission from the client.

You may also wish to take note of the appropriate limitation period before deciding when to destroy the file and what if anything from the file you should retain, whether as an original or a copy.

Certain papers such as attendance notes and copy emails may later help to explain why certain actions were taken.

Prior to any destruction of papers relating to the making of the will and its associated advice you should consider *Larke* v *Nugus* [2000] WTLR 1033. For more information see the Law Society's practice note on Disputed wills.

See 8.1.1 Practice notes.

If you destroy the file, you should keep a note with the will, so the absence of papers can be explained at a later stage to show that the destruction was carried out in accordance with good business practice.

4.4.1   If the client has made a new will

Even where you know or suspect that a client has made a new will, it is still possible that the validity of a subsequent will could be challenged so you should undertake a risk assessment of whether supporting documentation should be destroyed or copies kept where the originals have been sent to the client.

If the supporting documentation is to be destroyed you should advise the client that all supporting papers will be destroyed unless claimed and then keep a record of this notice.

4.4.2   If you cannot contact the client

If you cannot contact your client then you should document your efforts to trace the client and carry out a review before deciding whether to retain or destroy material.

You may wish to consider passing very old documents to a local authority archive as an alternative to destruction, but note the position regarding client confidentiality or legal privilege, in 6 below.

4.4.3   If the date of death is not known

The National Archives recommends that where personal data needs to be stored for the life of the relevant individual and the date of death is not known it should be held until that individual would have reached 100 years of age.

4.5   Documents relating to the death of the first spouse or civil partner

For deaths on or after 9 October 2007, spouses and civil partners can transfer any unused Inheritance Tax nil rate band allowances. This means that any part of the nil rate band that was not used when the spouse or civil partner died can be transferred to the second spouse or civil partner for use on their death.

The transfer of unused nil rate band applies only on the death of the second spouse or civil partner, so there is no need to agree the amount that is transferable on the first death.

You will need to retain full details of the estate of the first spouse or civil partner so that the information will be available for the second spouse or civil partner. This information comprises:

- a copy of the IHT400, IHT405 (C5 in Scotland) or full written details of the assets in the estate and their values;
- death certificate of the first spouse/civil partner;
- marriage or civil partnership certificate for the couple;
- copy of the grant of representation (Confirmation in Scotland);
- copy of the will, if there was one;
- a note of how the estate passed if there was no will;
- a copy of any Deed of Variation or other similar document if one was executed to change the people who inherited the state;
- any valuation(s) of assets that passed under will or intestacy other than to the surviving spouse or civil partner;
- the value of any other assets that also passed on the death of the first spouse or civil partner, for example jointly owned assets, assets held in trust and gifts made in the seven years prior to death;
- any evidence to support the availability of relief (such as agricultural or business relief) where the relievable assets pass to someone other than to the surviving spouse or civil partner.

For more information see HMRC guidance on Transferring an unused Inheritance Tax threshold.

5 STORING FILES

5.1 Electronic storage

The same issues arise with electronic data as with other material, so you always need to consider limitation periods, ownership, confidentiality, privilege and make an adequate risk assessment prior to destruction. However electronic data is subject to further regulatory safeguards as set out in the Data Protection Act 1998.

See 8.1.2 Legislation for further details.

5.1.1 Data protection

The Data Protection Act 1998 allows you to retain personal data stored in an office or the information on file without breaching the Act for as long as necessary for one or more specified lawful purposes.

Personal data contained within files in paper format are subject to the Act only if they are held in a relevant filing system (*Durant* v *Financial Services Authority* [2003] EWCA Civ 1747. See 8.1.3 Case law).

All personal data which are held in electronic format, including scanned documents which were formerly held in hard copy form, are subject to the Act.

For more information see the Law Society's practice note on Data protection in 8.1.1 Practice notes.

5.1.2 Data security

It is much easier to corrupt electronic data, whether by accident or design, than paper. Systems need to be in place to safeguard the authenticity, reliability, accessibility and security of all electronic material.

Email is both unreliable and an insecure medium. If necessary, encryption should be used to safeguard the confidentiality of information transmitted via email. Email should not be relied upon as a storage medium.

Information should be stored in a system, whether paper or electronic, which manages it according to its function and content, not its format.

For more information see the Law Society's practice note on Information security in 8.1.1 Practice notes.

5.1.3 Migrating data

It is a mistake to treat all data as though it were of equal value. Only business critical data or data of clear reference value should be migrated to new systems; the remainder should be destroyed according to an agreed retention and disposal policy prior to any migration occurring.

This is particularly important where personal data is concerned, since migration is a form of processing and should therefore not be undertaken if there is no longer any need to retain the data.

Migration of large quantities of data is additionally a costly process and can also result in loss or corruption of data elements. Before data is transferred to a new system, the firm should consider whether or not data is likely to be corrupted by the migration process.

5.2   Charges for storage

Your retainer should set out any charges for storage and for copying the file or producing a document from storage.

You may wish to remind your client that there is a cost to your business for storage and retrieval of documents from deep storage, particularly where the material is kept off site.

5.3   Storing files on microfilm

You may need your client's permission if you wish to put records of documents they own on microfilm, and you may wish to deal with such questions in your retainer letter as a matter of routine.

5.4   Losing a file

Loss of a file may amount to inadequate professional service or negligence where deeds are lost. You may need to contact your insurer to record the loss and you should consider contacting your client to discuss what remedial action can be taken, especially if original papers such as wills have been lost.

If a claim arises in relation to lost papers the courts will weigh up the available evidence to assess your part in the matter.

6   LIMITATION PERIODS

The limitation period may vary depending on the type of work undertaken.

6.1   Will files

When considering whether a file should be destroyed you should note that in will cases successful claims can be brought well after the usual contractual period of six years from the end of the retainer or time the work was completed/applicable in many other matters. Files should therefore be retained until any risk of a claim has passed.

Section 14B of the Limitation Act 1980 provides that a negligence claim will be time-barred after 15 years from the date on which the act or omission constituting negligence occurred, even where the cause of action has not yet accrued. There is no definition of negligence for this purpose so it is unclear whether 'negligence' is limited to the tort of negligence or whether it also includes a breach of contractual duty to exercise reasonable care and skill. There is judicial authority (*Societe Commerciale de Reassurance* v *ERAS (International) Ltd* [1992] 2 All ER 82) that in section 14A of the Limitation Act 1980 'negligence' is limited to the tort of negligence. Section 14B therefore may not be a complete protection against liability.

6.2   Personal representatives

For claims against personal representatives the limitation period is twelve years from the date on which the right to receive the property accrues (section 22(a) Limitation Act 1980) or from the date the right to receive the share accrued which may be from the end of the executors' year rather than the date of death. See 8.1.2 Legislation for details.

6.3   Discoverability – fraud mistake and concealment

Under section 32 of the Limitation Act 1980 the limitation period does not start to run until the claimant discovers the mistake, fraud or concealment or could have discovered it with reasonable diligence.

6.4 Disability/undue influence

Note that the limitation period, whichever applies, may not start to run until a claimant, deemed to have been under a disability (for example a minor child, a person with capacity problems, or someone suffering undue influence) has become free of that disability. So, for example, where a cause of action is apparent, a minor child will have six years from the date of attaining 18 years to take action.

Remember that a standard six year limitation period may not protect you in will related cases where, for example, undue influence is alleged, and note that in *Humphreys* v *Humphreys* [2004] EWHC 2201 (CH) a lifetime gift case, there was a successful challenge 13 years after the transaction. See 8.1.3 Case law for details.

7 HOW DOES CONFIDENTIALITY AND LEGAL PROFESSIONAL PRIVILEGE APPLY?

7.1 Confidentiality

The personal representatives will also decide whether to disclose any information to beneficiaries.

An executor's powers derive from the will, whereas an administrator's powers derive from the grant of representation. Accordingly, if the client died intestate, the administrator's authority to waive confidentiality will date from the issue of the grant.

There is an exception in cases where the validity of the will is in dispute. In such a case, the solicitor who prepared the will should make available a statement of his or her evidence regarding the execution of the will, and the circumstances surrounding it, regardless of whether or not the solicitor is acting for those named as executors in the will.

The statement should be available to anyone who is a party to probate proceedings or whom the solicitor believes has a reasonable claim under the will.

For more information see the Law Society's Disputed wills practice note in 8.1.1 Practice notes.

7.2 Privilege

'Legal advice privilege' protects a client's communications to and from his lawyer made for the purpose of seeking legal advice or assistance.

Legal privilege belongs to the client, and only he/she can waive it. Privilege of the client passes to the personal representatives on death.

8 FURTHER INFORMATION

8.1 References

8.1.1 Practice notes

- Information security
- Data protection
- Anti-money laundering
- Disputed wills
- Making gifts of assets

8.1.2   Legal and statutory regulations

- Inheritance (Provision for Family and Dependants) Act 1975
- Money Laundering Regulations 2007
- Value Added Tax Act 1994
- Data Protection Act 1998
- Limitation Act 1980

8.1.3   Cases

- *Durant* v *Financial Services Authority* [2003] EWCA Civ 1746
- *Humphreys* v *Humphreys* [2004] EWHC 2201 (CH)
- *Larke* v *Nugus* (2000) WTLR 1033

8.2   Practice Advice

The Law Society provides support to solicitors on a wide range of areas of legal practice. The service is staffed by solicitors and can be contacted on 0870 606 2522 from 09.00 to 17.00 on weekdays.

Visit the Practice Advice Service website.

8.3   Further products and support

8.3.1   Law Society publications

- *Lasting Powers of Attorney*, 2nd Ed
- *Probate Practitioner's Handbook*, 6th Ed
- *Elderly Client Handbook*, 4th Ed

8.3.2   Training and events

- CPD course: Tips on drafting wills for business owners (webinar)

   [http://cpdengage.com/clients/law/course/2697/tips-on-drafting-wills-for-business-owners]

8.4   Acknowledgements

The Law Society acknowledges the contribution of the Wills and Equity Committee in drafting this guidance.

Financial abuse practice note

13 June 2013 .

1   INTRODUCTION

1.1   Who should read this practice note?

All solicitors who advise clients that are or may be at risk of financial abuse, in particular those conducting private client work involving financial planning, execution of wills or LPAs.

1.2   What is the issue?

As a result of economic recession, social change and advances in technology the risk of financial abuse is increasing. Solicitors are well placed to identify possible or actual financial abuse in the context of particular retainers.

You have a responsibility to be aware of financial abuse and to understand your role in both preventing it and taking action to protect clients who have been financially abused.

Financial abuse covers a wide variety of activities from mishandling finances to fraud, but may broadly be described as a violation of an individual's rights relating to their financial affairs or assets.

Anyone can be a victim of financial abuse, but particular groups may be especially at risk. Age and specific disabilities may have an impact on the individual's capacity to make decisions which places them at increased risk of abuse.

People with learning disabilities or other conditions that have led to cognitive impairment, and in some instances, people who have poor mental health may also be particularly at risk.

This practice note is aimed to assist you in identifying and acting upon suspected or actual financial abuse in the course of your practice.

The SRA has published a Handbook, which sets out all the SRA's regulatory requirements. It outlines the ethical standards that the SRA expects of law firms and practitioners and the outcomes that the SRA expects them to achieve for their clients.

An overview of outcomes-focused regulation (OFR) can be found on the Law Society's website. This provides information on what the SRA Handbook contains, including a summary of the chapters in the Code of Conduct and a summary of the reporting requirements included throughout the Handbook.

1.3   Professional conduct

The following sections of the SRA Code are relevant to this issue:

- Chapter 1 on Client Care
- Chapter 4 on Confidentiality and disclosure
- Chapter 11 on Relations with third parties

1.4   Status

Practice notes are issued by the Law Society for the use and benefit of its members. They represent the Law Society's view of good practice in a particular area. They are not intended to be the only standard of good practice that solicitors can follow. You are not required to follow them, but doing so will make it easier to account to oversight bodies for your actions.

Practice notes are not legal advice, nor do they necessarily provide a defence to complaints of misconduct or of inadequate professional service. While care has been taken to ensure that they are accurate, up to date and useful, the Law Society will not accept any legal liability in relation to them.

For queries or comments on this practice note, contact the Law Society's Practice Advice Service: **www.lawsociety.org.uk/practiceadvice**.

1.5   Terminology

Must

A specific requirement in legislation or of a principle, rule, outcome or other mandatory provision in the SRA Handbook. You must comply, unless there are specific exemptions or defences provided for in relevant legislation or the SRA Handbook.

Should

- Outside of a regulatory context, good practice for most situations in the Law Society's view.
- In the case of the SRA Handbook, an indicative behaviour or other non-mandatory provision (such as may be set out in notes or guidance).

These may not be the only means of complying with legislative or regulatory requirements and there may be situations where the suggested route is not the best possible route to meet the needs of your client. However, if you do not follow the suggested route, you should be able to justify to oversight bodies why the alternative approach you have taken is appropriate, either for your practice, or in the particular retainer.

May

A non-exhaustive list of options for meeting your obligations or running your practice. Which option you choose is determined by the profile of the individual practice, client or retainer. You may be required to justify why this was an appropriate option to oversight bodies.

2   SRA PRINCIPLES

There are ten mandatory principles which apply to all those the SRA regulates and to all aspects of practice. The principles can be found in the SRA Handbook.

When thinking about how to meet the outcomes in the Code/Handbook, you must consider the principles which apply across the Handbook including the Code. You should always bear in mind what the ten principles are and use them as your starting point when implementing the outcomes.

3 FINANCIAL ABUSE

3.1 What is financial abuse?

There is no statutory definition of financial abuse. However, statutory guidance published by the Department of Health entitled 'No Secrets' defines financial abuse as follows:

> Financial or material abuse, including theft, fraud, exploitation, pressure in connection with wills, property or inheritance or financial transactions, or the misuse or misappropriation of property, possessions or benefits. (DH/Home Office, 2000)

More information about 'No Secrets' can be found in 7.3.1 Codes of practice.

3.2 Forms of financial abuse

'No Secrets' is the English guidance to local authorities on safeguarding, and it identifies financial or material abuse as including a range of activities, which are listed below with examples of how they might manifest in practice.

In Wales, the applicable guidance is 'In Safe Hands', and for cross-border cases, it should be noted that the Scottish legislative regime is different.

- **theft** – either physically, or through transfer of funds from the vulnerable person
- **misappropriation or misuse of money or property** – for example, improper use of money or assets when handling it for a vulnerable person under informal arrangements
- **exerting undue influence to give away assets or gifts** – this can include placing inappropriate pressure on a vulnerable person to change their will, or make gifts they otherwise would not or signing over the family home to one relative when the older person is about to go into residential care
- **putting undue pressure on the older person to accept lower-cost/lower-quality services** in order to preserve more financial resources to be passed to beneficiaries on death
- **carrying out unnecessary work and/or overcharging** – for example, tradesmen advising repairs for non-existent problems to property, or offering a service such as will writing accompanied by pressure selling, work for which is overcharged, and/or charged in advance
- **misuse of older persons' assets by professionals** – for example, by accountants or legal professionals with access to client funds
- **misuse of enduring/lasting powers of attorney** – use other than as intended or further than as limited by the document
- **misuse of welfare benefits** by appointees appointed to manage such benefits on behalf of a person lacking capacity to manage them
- **misuse of Direct Payments** by paid carers or family members instead of using the money for the benefit of the recipient
- **salesmen encouraging certain people with learning disabilities who may lack capacity for their finances to enter into contracts or changing suppliers** (for example for mobile phone services) when they do not understand their contractual responsibilities. This can also arise with older people, who may have limited capability to understand such contracts
- **apparent theft or loss of possessions**, for example in contexts such as hospitals or care homes, or where people have carers at home.

Assumptions that a person is fully protected once in these contexts should be avoided, as they can remain vulnerable to any of the above forms of abuse.

4 IDENTIFICATION OF ADULTS VULNERABLE TO ABUSE AND PRECAUTIONS TO BE TAKEN

4.1 Groups at particular risk

Although anyone can be the victim of financial abuse, certain groups are particularly at risk.

4.1.1 Older people

In particular, older people are extremely vulnerable to financial abuse whether perpetrated by relatives, carers or strangers.

You should not assume that any person accompanying your client has their best interests at heart. You should be alert to the nature of the instructions you receive and the manner or behaviour of someone who accompanies the client.

A study found the following factors predispose an older person to financial abuse. This is not an exhaustive list and some factors may apply to persons other than older people:

- advanced age
- stroke
- dementia or other cognitive impairment
- physical, mental or emotional distress
- depression
- recent loss of spouse or divorce
- social isolation
- middle or upper income bracket
- taking multiple medications
- frailty.

More information on the study, 'Strategy for Recognising, Preventing and Dealing with the Abuse of Older and Vulnerable People', Solicitors for the Elderly, January 2010 can be found at section 7.3.3.

You may also need to consider a client's background in order to assess their capability. For example, some older women may not have had an involvement in the family finances, so a partner's death can have a greater impact on their capability than is immediately evident.

4.1.2 Other vulnerable adults

While older people may be particularly vulnerable other groups may also be vulnerable to financial abuse, including individuals with learning disabilities, poor mental health and acquired brain injury (eg stroke).

People with sensory impairments may also be at particular risk of abuse, especially where they are relying on others for information and assistance managing their affairs.

Government guidance and case law commonly cite the Law Commission Report *Who decides?: making decisions on behalf of mentally incapacitated adults* (1997) when defining 'vulnerable adults'.

Under this definition, a vulnerable adult is a person over 18 years of age who:

> is or may be in need of community care services by reason of mental or other disability, age or illness and who is or may be unable to take care himself or herself, or unable to protect himself or herself against significant harm or serious exploitation.

More information can be found at 7.5.1 Law Commission Report.

The Law Society acknowledges the view of many stakeholders that use of the word 'vulnerable' can be perceived as negative and can undermine the fact that the fault of any abuse lies solely with the perpetrator.

'Vulnerable adults' has been used in this document only for clarity as the existing legal term used in applicable guidance, and is only intended to refer to people at greater risk of financial abuse.

Capacity can fluctuate over time alongside other circumstances such mental health problems, and you should therefore assess capacity at the point a decision is being made by the client.

People with fluctuating mental health conditions may be aware that their capacity to instruct and to manage their financial affairs can vary, and may want advice to help them plan for times when they lack capacity. See section 4.3.2 on 'Capacity to instruct a solicitor' for further details.

4.2   What to be alert for – known indicators for abusive activity

Financial abuse indicators can include the following scenarios and even though these indicators have been set out for elderly persons, they can also be found in financial abuse of other client groups such as people with learning disability etc:

- signatures on cheques, or other documents that do not resemble the vulnerable person's signature or are signed when the person is unable to write
- any sudden changes in bank accounts, including unexplained withdrawals of large sums of money by a person accompanying the vulnerable person
- the sudden inclusion of additional names on an vulnerable person's bank accounts or benefits payments – often these individuals are unrelated to the older person
- abrupt changes to or creation of wills that leave most or all of the assets to a new friend or only one relative
- the sudden appearance of previously uninvolved relatives claiming their rights to a vulnerable person's affairs and possessions
- unexplained sudden transfers of assets to a family member or someone outside the family
- numerous small sums of cash being 'given' to, or money regularly disappearing after visits from a relative or neighbour
- numerous unpaid bills when someone else is supposed to be paying bills for the vulnerable person
- unusual concern by someone that an excessive amount of money is being expended on the care of the vulnerable person
- lack of amenities such as TV, personal grooming items, appropriate clothing items, that the vulnerable person should be able to afford
- the unexplained disappearance of funds or valuables such as jewellery
- deliberate isolation of a vulnerable person from their friends and family, resulting in the carer alone having total control.

From *A Strategy for Recognising, Preventing and Dealing with the Abuse of Older and Vulnerable People*, Solicitors for the Elderly, January 2010. See further information at 7.3.3 Third party guidance.

While solicitors may be more likely to notice some indicators than others, depending on the nature of their practice (for example, with regard to will making, gifts or transfer of assets), they may also become aware of others during the course of their work for a client.

Mental health awareness training and disability equality training can assist in identifying potential abuse. You may wish to dedicate some of your CPD hours to such courses to develop this awareness.

4.3 Identification and the assessment of capacity

Clients who may exhibit particular vulnerability to financial abuse may also lack capacity to provide instructions for a transaction.

Clients who lack capacity may be at greater risk of abuse; for example, they may not understand the risks and consequences of making a substantial gift of their assets or of transferring their family home into the names of relatives.

Solicitors are service providers under equality legislation and you should use plain English when speaking or writing to the client about measures that would protect them from abuse.

If your client does lack capacity, then your role and obligations are different to when the client has capacity. The assessment of mental capacity is governed by the Mental Capacity Act 2005 (MCA 2005).

4.3.1 *Principles*

The MCA 2005 sets out a number of principles for its application, the first three of which act as a starting point for assessing capacity:

- A person must be assumed to have capacity unless it is established that he lacks capacity – Section 1(2)
- A person is not to be treated as unable to make a decision unless all practicable steps to help him to do so have been taken without success – Section 1(3)
- A person is not to be treated as unable to make a decision merely because he makes an unwise decision – Section 1(4)

The MCA 2005 Code of Practice provides a comprehensive explanation of how these principles are applied.

4.3.2 *Capacity to instruct the solicitor*

If you are in any doubt as to whether a client has capacity to provide instructions, you must perform a capacity assessment before any instructions are acted upon.

The assessment should be conducted with the client alone without other family members being present. It should not be assumed that anyone accompanying the client has their best interests at heart.

However, it may be useful to observe how any relative or friend who has accompanied the client behaves towards the client and vice versa to identify whether there is the possibility of undue influence or pressure.

Section 2(1) of the MCA sets out a two stage test for establishing a lack of capacity, explained in the Code of Practice as determining whether:

- they have an impairment or disturbance (for example, a disability, condition or trauma) that affects the way their mind or brain works, and
- the impairment or disturbance means that they are unable to make a specific decision at the time it needs to be made.

Further information can be found at See 7.3.1 Codes of practice.

An impairment or disturbance can be temporary, and the relevant time for establishing whether one exists is the time the decision needs to be made.

For a person to lack capacity to make a specific decision, it must be established on the balance of probabilities that they are unable:

- to understand the information relevant to the decision, or;

- to retain the information, or;
- to use or weigh up the information as part of the process of making the decision, or
- to communicate the decision (whether by talking, sign language, or any other means).

Most importantly, section 3(4) states that the information relevant to a decision includes information about the reasonably foreseeable consequences of deciding one way or the other or failing to make a decision.

This provision is useful for assessing people with borderline or fluctuating capacity. If the person fails any one of the elements listed above, then they are treated as lacking capacity for that decision.

4.3.3   MCA 2005 and undue influence or misuse of power

Under MCA 2005, there remain a number of decisions where case law determines whether or not the person has the capacity to decide a matter.

This includes capacity to make a will (*Banks* v *Goodfellow* (1870) LR 5 QB 549) and capacity to instruct a solicitor to take legal proceedings (*Masterman-Lister* v *Brutton & Co* [2002] EWCA Civ 1889).

There are a minority of cases where a person may appear to have capacity under the MCA 2005 test but actually lacks capacity when they come under pressure from powerful relatives or friends. This can happen for example, to someone in the early stages of dementia or with a mild learning disability.

In *DL* v *A Local Authority & Ors* [2012] EWCA Civ 253 the Court of Appeal used its inherent jurisdiction to protect such vulnerable adults.

Since then, the inherent jurisdiction has been used infrequently to protect this group of people.

Further steps in assessing capacity

In addition to the principles set out at the start of this section, the following list provides a summary of the relevant issues and actions you should bear in mind when assessing capacity.

The threshold test for establishing lack of capacity will vary depending on the seriousness of the decision being made, which for example may be of a different level when making a will, gift or lasting power of attorney.

Similarly, the formality of the assessment should relate to the seriousness of the decision. The assessment of capacity form (COP3) requires the form to be completed by a 'practitioner', which could be a psychologist, psychiatrist, or other registered medical practitioner. In some circumstances it can be signed by a registered therapist such as a speech therapist or occupational therapist.

When choosing a health professional to conduct a capacity assessment of your client, you should make sure he or she has a good understanding of the Mental Capacity Act.

While there is an assumption of capacity under the MCA principles, you must be satisfied that the client has the requisite capacity to provide a given instruction.

You should not express a view on a client's capacity before conducting a formal assessment with them.

You should be careful to distinguish between the ability to express a choice (eg one beneficiary over another) and the capacity to understand the consequences and effects of a transaction involving the client's own interests. Under the MCA principles above, their choice does not have to be a wise one or one that you agree with.

If the client's capacity is in doubt, you should obtain a medical or other expert opinion (relevant to the matter affecting the client's capacity) when making the assessment of capacity in relation to specific decisions. This could be a specialist medical opinion, eg from a psychiatrist or geriatrician, a psychologist specialising in learning disability, or a neuro-psychiatrist or neuro-psychologist for a person with an acquired brain injury.

Your client might have had contact with local authority social services who may have already completed a pro forma assessment of capacity for the relevant issue. This should be shared free of charge with you upon request (subject to your client's consent) and provides a good reference point in deciding whether or not it will be necessary to proceed to arrange a further professional opinion on your client's capacity.

Where social care or minor financial decisions are involved, such as a decision to move into residential care, or relating to contact with certain family members, a capacity assessment form can be completed by the local authority social worker.

For treatment decisions or major financial decisions, you may prefer to consult the treating psychiatrist, rehabilitation consultant or general practitioner. You should approach medical or social professionals who know the client well, especially if the client presents as if they have capacity, but appears unduly influenced or intimidated when in the presence of a particular relative.

The Law Society and British Medical Association book *Assessment of Mental Capacity* (3rd Edition) provides guidance on how lawyers and health and social care professionals can ensure this process is thorough and best ensures the protection of your client.

You should be aware of Data Protection Act obligations and the Solicitors' Code of Conduct when seeking medical or other opinions More information about the data protection act can be found 7.3.2.

What happens when someone lacks capacity

If a person lacks capacity to make a decision, then the best interests principle applies.

Those close to the family should be consulted, and the views and wishes of the person lacking capacity should be taken into account before family or professionals can proceed to make a best interests decision on behalf of the person (see s5 of the MCA 2005).

You should continue to consult and involve a person who lacks capacity to instruct in decisions and further steps to be taken. Ensuring that a person has an independent advocate can assist in this regard.

Any substantial financial transaction will require Court of Protection involvement if the client lacks capacity (see sections below on Powers of Attorneys and deputyship).

However, if you determine on your own assessment that it appears the client lacks capacity to instruct you, then you should discuss the need to obtain a formal assessment of capacity from a relevant professional with your client.

5   TAKING ACTION TO PREVENT ABUSE

If you suspect financial abuse, deciding on the appropriate action will not always be a straightforward decision. This is especially so when taking into account the rules of client confidentiality.

If your client does not have capacity to make the relevant decision or take the action that they want to take, then arguably your duty of care to protect that person in the public interest has to be weighed against the duty of confidentiality.

It is important to work and plan together with a client to prevent financial abuse, for example by taking precautionary measures to protect against financial abuse during periods when the client anticipates they may be unwell.

This could include:

- making an LPA
- making arrangements for two signatures to be required for withdrawal of sums above a certain amount.

These planning decisions need to be taken carefully, and balanced against the risk of the client being exposed to a greater risk of financial abuse (for example, by their attorney).

If you have a reasonable belief that an offence has been committed against your client and you have their consent to notify the police and other appropriate authorities you should do so.

Other methods of protecting your client from financial abuse are detailed in the sections below.

5.1 Powers of attorney

Lasting powers of attorney (which continue to be valid after the person loses capacity, unlike a power of attorney) enable an adult to appoint a third party to exercise decision-making powers on behalf of the donor.

It is important that clients understand the risks as well as the benefits of granting these powers, and you should be aware of the potential for their abuse and build in appropriate safeguards.

You should take special care if a client arrives with a new friend or long lost relative who they wish to nominate as their financial attorney, particularly when there is a complex portfolio of assets or large assets.

This person may be taking advantage of the client. In this situation you may decide to enquire into the nature of the relationship with the client. Such a decision will be within your professional judgement and may assist in ascertaining whether the relationship is genuine or not, and that the instructions are in the interests of the client.

You should note that a specific capacity test applies to making a lasting power of attorney.

The same principles apply to enduring powers of attorney executed before the implementation of the MCA, as these are still lawful.

For further information on lasting powers of attorney, including client's capacity to make them, and building in safeguards against abuse, solicitors should refer to the Law Society Lasting powers of attorney practice note.

5.2 Gifts

Clients should be made aware of the nature of any gift as an outright transfer, and should be made aware of the risks any substantial transfers may increase regarding their ability to support themselves independently.

Potential beneficiaries of the client's will, such as family members, may have encouraged the client to make a gift in order to avoid taxes or nursing home fees.

As well as advising the client of the risks to their future independence that such gifts might entail, it may not be an effective way to avoid tax.

Further, the local authority may treat this gift as a deliberate deprivation of assets for the purpose of avoiding paying residential or nursing home fees, which results in the local authority charging full fees to the client.

For further information on gifts of assets, solicitors should refer to the Law Society Making gifts of assets practice note.

5.3 Wills

When drafting wills, you should be particularly alert for potential abuse in the following instances:

- where the person making the will is not being allowed individual access to you
- where instructions come from a third party
- where instructions are coming from a third party who is to benefit from the will
- where a third party is always present at an interview with the solicitor

- where a third party is using their own solicitor to prepare a will for a vulnerable person who has previously had their own solicitor.

5.4   Estate administration

You should always be aware of the potential for abuse where an elderly person wishes to appoint an attorney for the purposes of taking out a grant of probate or letters of administration.

Notice should also be taken of substantial 'interference' or influence where a third party is becoming involved in the administration of an unconnected person's estate where they do not benefit or have no indirect benefit.

5.5   Mis-selling

Some groups at particular risk may lack capacity for their finances to enter into contracts, to change suppliers or to understand their contractual responsibilities.

If you suspect your client has been mis-sold a product or service, you may wish to consider approaching the relevant ombudsman. For example, for mis-selling of financial products, you or the client can contact the Financial Ombudsman. More information about the Financial Ombudsman can be found at 7.4.2 Financial ombudsman.

5.6   Language and cultural barriers

You should take great care to correctly identify the relationship between clients and any person accompanying them.

The exact nature of relationships can become confused when interpretation is necessary for communication with the client, or where the client is from a cultural background that identifies such relationships differently (for example, using familial language to describe someone not formally related to the client).

If you are concerned that the client's wishes are not being communicated accurately by someone that they have elected to translate for them, you should consider whether to engage an independent translator.

It is also important to ensure that contractual terms and consequences are clearly understood by clients from cultural backgrounds that may hold different understandings of contractual and propriety concepts.

6   ADDRESSING SUSPECTED ABUSE – WHAT STEPS TO TAKE

6.1   Confidentiality

General guidance on the common law of confidentiality, data protection and freedom of information principles is available in *SCIE Report 50: Safeguarding adults at risk of harm and No Secrets*.

It is important to note that guidance available on confidentiality has been substantially reduced under the new SRA Code. Chapter 4, Outcome 1 requires that:

> the affairs of the clients are kept confidential by you and your firm unless disclosure is required by or permitted by law or the client consents;

There are no specific exceptions to this outcome in the Code that relate to permitting disclosure so as to protect a client without capacity from abuse committed by a third party, nor does the code detail any relevant indicative behaviours. The Law Society is currently seeking to address this shortfall in protection for clients.

For advice on the Code of Conduct, solicitors should call the SRA professional ethics helpline on 0870 606 2577.

Solicitors may also find it useful to review the ICO guidance on disclosure under the Data Protection Act and the OPG Safeguarding Policy on sharing of information (section 7.3.2 below).

6.2   Office of the Public Guardian

The Office of the Public Guardian (OPG) has responsibility for investigating concerns about the actions of registered attorneys and deputies (or where the Court has authorised an action under a single order).

It has an investigations unit with a dedicated phone number which can be found at section 7.4.1 below. Its Safeguarding Vulnerable Adults policy outlines what they can do if investigating any of the above.

It could take any of the following actions:

- apply to the Court for the **suspension, discharge or replacement of a deputy**
- apply to the Court for an **Order to be varied or for a deputy's security bond to be called in or varied**
- apply to the Court for a **revocation of a power of attorney**
- inform the **police**, where a crime may have been committed
- require a deputy to **provide a final report** where the person he or she was acting for has died or the deputy has been discharged
- monitor the situation through ongoing close **supervision** of the deputy in the case
- inform **external agencies**. This will include notifying any professional body, where the perpetrator is a member, and the Independent Safeguarding Authority (from October 2009).

The OPG policy sets the following time limits for local authorities:

- same-day referral to adult social care teams or relevant outside organisations
- the next day for any decision to investigate, and
- five working days to formulate a multi-agency plan for assessing the risk and addressing any immediate protection needs.

In practice, if the local authority have already placed the vulnerable adult into safeguarding, and are planning legal action against the suspected abuser, the OPG and the local authority will work together to decide which agency will take the lead for action.

If there are concerns about a person who is outside of the scope of an OPG investigation, the policy states that the informant should always be told:

- when the OPG's action has completed, or
- when the matter has been referred to another agency for investigation, and
- if it has been referred, who it has been referred to.

More information about persons outside the scope can be found in 6.2.1.

There may be situations where the person subject to abuse lacks capacity but the Public Guardian lacks jurisdiction to intervene as they do not have an appointed deputy or attorney.

In these circumstances you may want to consider or advise on an application to the court. The court has wide powers which may be exercised to protect someone who lacks capacity. This includes powers to appoint a deputy, make declarations of capacity, or prohibit named persons from contacting someone who lacks capacity.

The Government is consulting on legislation in response to the Law Commission's report on the review of Adult Social Care law, which contained a number of proposals on safeguarding.

You should remain alert to any changes in this area of law.

6.2.1 *Examples of persons outside the scope of the OPG*

An unregistered EPA

The OPG will normally make a referral to the Adult Social Care Department of the local authority of the area where the vulnerable person lives. If the donor of the EPA lacks capacity to make decisions, the OPG may advise that an application is made to the Court of Protection for revocation of the EPA and the appointment of a deputy. The court will sometimes order the Public Guardian to provide a report under Section 49 of the Mental Capacity Act in such cases.

A former receiver or deputy

The OPG will normally advise the current deputy to deal with the matter. Where a deputy has been discharged, or has died, or the vulnerable adult has died, the OPG can call for a final report from the former deputy (or the personal representatives if the deputy has died). If the Public Guardian is not satisfied, he may apply to the Court of Protection for enforcement of the security bond. This only applies to deaths/discharges after 1 October 2007.

Any other person

The OPG will make a referral to Adult Social Care and if the vulnerable adult has an appointed deputy then the OPG will want to be kept informed of the situation and could contribute to the action by monitoring the situation through supervision of the deputy and visits to the vulnerable adult from a Court of Protection Visitor.

Appointees

The OPG will make a referral to the Department for Work and Pensions and to Adult Social Care.

6.3 Litigation

If litigation is contemplated, you should consult with family members to see if an appropriate individual is able to act as a litigation friend.

If there is no family or no one who does not present a potential conflict of interest with the client, e.g. the relative is the suspected abuser, then you should contact the Official Solicitor. The Official Solicitor can be appointed as litigation friend, if proceedings need to be taken.

6.4 Deputyship

If the client has assets that need protecting and lacks capacity to manage their assets, an application should be made to the Court of Protection for a deputy to be appointed.

The Court will give wide ranging powers to the deputy to manage the client's bank accounts, sell property, and manage other assets.

If there is a need for a court order appointing a deputy, then if no suitable individual can be found or no relative is willing to act as deputy, or you do not provide such a service, then one option would be to contact the local authority's adult care solicitor to ask whether the local authority Deputyship team is willing to act as deputy.

Failing this, an application can be made for a 'panel deputy' to be appointed.

A panel deputy is a member of an approved list of deputies (mostly solicitors) with specialist knowledge of the MCA 2005.

A list of panel deputies can be found on the justice.gov website, and the Court of Protection has access to a Panel of Deputies who may be called on where there is no-one else willing or able to take on the role of deputy.

You should consider whether it is appropriate for an application to be made for a statutory will.

6.5 Appointeeship

If a client is in receipt of a state pension and/or benefits, an application can be made to the Department of Works and Pensions for a suitable relative to be appointed as the appointee of the client's benefits if:

- the client does not have capacity to manage them any longer, or
- there are concerns that these are being mismanaged.

If there is no relative or no suitable relative, then the local authority may agree to be appointed as appointee of the benefits and pension.

If you have concerns that the benefits are being mismanaged, then you should consider reporting these concerns to the Department of Works and Pensions who will investigate whether or not the current appointee is a suitable person to continue to act as appointee.

You can contact the Pensions Service on 0845 6060265 for those over 60 if they suspect abuse and want to apply for appointeeship.

For those under 60 there are a number of potential remedies and the contact number is 0845 6088506.

The DWP benefit fraud hotline can be contacted on 0800 854 440. There is also a DLA and Attendance Allowance hotline which can be contacted on 08457 123456.

On contacting these hotlines, you will be informed of the appropriate office to send a fax with a letter and/or application to take over appointeeship or report concerns.

6.6 The role of the local authority

Under *No Secrets*, the lead agency responsible for arranging safeguarding procedures to take protective action for a vulnerable adult is the local authority adult care department.

The local authority can arrange an initial strategy meeting which is attended by relevant professionals, both statutory and voluntary, dealing with the vulnerable adult with a view to deciding immediate measures to prevent or stop the financial abuse.

Later, a case conference will be held to examine the effectiveness of the measures and decide further strategies.

It is important that the vulnerable adult's capacity to make relevant decisions, such as decisions to protect themselves against abuse, capacity to manage their finances and assets is assessed as soon as possible so that the outcome will determine the available legal options such as using the Court of Protection or not.

6.7 Abuse and neglect by legal professionals

If you suspect abuse or neglect by another legal professional, you should contact the SRA for guidance. For more information see 7.2.2.

6.8 Criminal offences

Where you suspect an appointee is not using their powers for the benefit of the vulnerable adult then you should notify the DWP.

If you suspect a criminal offence may be taking place, contact your local safeguarding team or the police. However, the police may ask that no action be taken while they investigate and gather evidence against the perpetrator before the perpetrator realises that the police are investigating.

The difficulty with this approach is that you may have a duty of care to apply for deputyship in the interim to protect the assets from being further dissipated by the perpetrator. If the perpetrator is a deputy or attorney, the OPG will want to launch an investigation.

Generally local authority solicitors will cooperate with the police. You should make clear that they must take interim steps to apply to the Court of Protection if there are sufficient assets to make it worthwhile appointing a deputyship. If not, they must notify DWP to stop paying the adult's benefits to the perpetrator as the appointee.

Local authorities may also be able to assist, by considering what protective action might be needed in cases of financial abuse; this action can include applying for interim deputyship orders or a single order.

7 FURTHER INFORMATION

7.1 Law Society

7.1.1 Law Society Practice Advice Service

The Law Society Practice Advice Service provides a dedicated support line for Law Society members and employees of law firms.

7.1.2 Law Society practice notes

- Making gifts of assets practice note
- Lasting powers of attorney practice note

7.1.3 Law Society publications

- Assessment of Mental Capacity, 3rd Edition (2009)
- Anti-Money Laundering Toolkit
- Lexcel Financial Management and Business Planning Toolkit

7.2 Solicitors Regulation Authority

7.2.1 Professional Ethics Helpline

Contact the Solicitors Regulation Authority's Professional ethics helpline for advice on conduct issues.

[**www.sra.org.uk/contactus.page**]

7.2.2 Reporting another professional

The SRA provides guidance reporting misconduct.

[**www.sra.org.uk/solicitors/enforcement/solicitor-report/other-solicitor-results.page**]

7.3 Guidance

7.3.1 Codes of practice

- *Mental Capacity Act 2005 Code of Practice*

- *No Secrets* – Department of Health and Home Office guidance on developing and implementing multi-agency policies and procedures to protect vulnerable adults from abuse (2010) (now on national archives website)
- *In Safe Hands* – Welsh Government guidance on adult protection procedures
- *SCIE Report 50: Safeguarding adults at risk of harm* – Social Care Institute for Excellence guidance on safeguarding which includes information on financial abuse against vulnerable adults (2011).

7.3.2   Data protection

- Information Commissioner guidance on disclosure
- ICO guidance on releasing information to prevent or detect crime (section 29), Data Protection Act
- OPG safeguarding policy on sharing of information, section 8.8

7.3.3   Third party guidance

A Strategy for Recognising, Preventing and Dealing with the Abuse of Older and Vulnerable People, Solicitors for the Elderly (January 2010)

7.4   Useful contacts

7.4.1   Office of the Public Guardian

Office of the Public Guardian Investigations Unit contact details, Policy Guidance, the Procedures and Practice Guidance and the Protocol for working with Local Authorities.

[www.justice.gov.uk/contacts/opg]

7.4.2   Other groups

- Action on Elder Abuse
- Age UK
- Financial Ombudsman
- Mencap
- Mind
- Office of the Public Guardian: OPG on Justice.gov and OPG on GOV.uk
- Solicitors for the Elderly

7.5   Other resources

7.5.1   Law Commission report

Law Commission report: 'Who decides?': making decisions on behalf of mentally incapacitated adults' (1997)

7.6   Acknowledgements

The Law Society acknowledges the Mental Health and Disability Committee for its help in developing this practice note.

The Law Society would like to express its gratitude to the following organisations for their assistance in reviewing the practice note:

- Action Against Elder Abuse
- Age UK
- ADASS
- The Local Government Association
- MIND
- The Office of the Public Guardian
- The Official Solicitor

Useful links

- **www.lawsociety.org.uk/advice/practice-notes/documents/financial-abuse-flow-chart-case-studies**

Law Society member benefits

Practices may be looking to commercial organisations for solutions to the challenges presented by implementation of the WIQS Core Practice Management Standards and the Wills and Inheritance Protocol. The Law Society has negotiated special discounts for its members with the following suppliers that may be relevant.

Supplier:	**BankersAccuity**
Description:	BankersAccuity is the world's leading provider of international payment routing data and anti-money laundering (AML) screening software, enabling organisations to maximise payment efficiency and ensure AML compliance.
Tel:	020 7653 3800
Email:	sales@bankersaccuity.com
Website:	www.accuitysolutions.com/legal

Supplier:	**Certainty**
Description:	The Certainty National Will Register and Will Search service has grown in response to demand from the legal profession and the public to register and search for wills. Certainty provides three core services: a national will register; will search services; and will management with integrated marketing.
Tel:	0845 408 0404
Email:	solicitors@certainty.co.uk
Website:	www.certainty.co.uk

Supplier	**Experian**
Description:	Experian is the leading global information services company and the Law Society's preferred supplier for AML e-verifications, identity and know your customer (KYC) checking. Practices can use identity verification to help satisfy customer due diligence requirements and money laundering regulations.
Tel:	0845 266 6604
Email:	info@experianidentityandfraud.com
Website:	www.experian.co.uk/identity-and-fraud/legal-sector/intro.html

Supplier: **JLT Property Insurance**

Description: JLT Property Insurance is the endorsed insurance partner of the Law Society, providing buildings, contents, property owner liability and legal expenses insurance for unoccupied properties, tailored specifically for probate solicitors.

Tel: 0800 316 9842

Email: unoccupiedproperty@jltgroup.com

Website: www.jltpropertyinsurance.co.uk

Supplier: **Riliance**

Description: Riliance is the market-leading online support tool for compliance officers for legal practice (COLPs) and compliance officers for finance and administration (COFAs). The web-based management system enables you to plan, delegate, audit and report your organisation's risk and compliance workload. It has been developed by risk and compliance experts who have worked in legal practice and understand the practicalities of meeting regulatory obligations.

Tel: 020 7320 5682

Email: riliancecompliance@lawsociety.org.uk

Website: www.riliance.co.uk

Supplier: **SIFA**

Description: The Society has endorsed the SIFA Directory of Professional Financial Advisers, which lists only advisers who are free of the influence of the providers of financial products and specialise in working with professionals. The Directory categorises financial advisers by reference to business specialisations which are relevant to solicitors, including trust and tax, later life, matrimonial, PI and Court of Protection.

Tel: 01372 721172

Email: ian.muirhead@sifa.co.uk

Website: http://legal.sifa.co.uk

Supplier: **Make It Cheaper** – business utility and telecoms bills

Description: The Law Society has partnered with Make It Cheaper, the UK's largest energy price comparison service exclusively for businesses. Make It Cheaper compares all suppliers for business utility bills and business telecoms and reads all the small print to save you money, time and hassle.

Tel: 0800 970 0077

Email: partnerships@makeitcheaper.com

Website: www.makeitcheaper.com

Supplier: **Moneypenny** – telephone answering and outsourced switchboard

Description: Moneypenny gives practices their own Moneypenny Receptionist. Fully briefed by the practice, the service will look after calls as if based in its office. Moneypenny offers support for an in-house team and gives you the choice of outsourcing a practice's switchboard entirely, or simply as part of your business continuity and disaster recovery plan. Moneypenny is a trading name of Callitech Ltd.

Tel: 0333 202 1005

Email: hello@moneypenny.co.uk

Website: www.moneypenny.co.uk/law-firms

Supplier: **Syscap** – Practising Certificate Spread Payment Facility

Description: Known as the UK's leading independent IT finance provider, Syscap also provides tailored finance solutions and advice to commercial, professional and public sector organisations. Syscap's Spread Payment Facility, endorsed by the Law Society, allows you to spread the cost of your practising certificate and regulatory fees over 10 equal monthly instalments.

Tel: 0208 254 1830

Email: spf@syscap.com

Website: www.syscap.com/professions/products-and-solutions/practising-certificates

Supplier: **Wincanton Records Management**

Description: Wincanton Records Management is a Law Society endorsed service that takes responsibility for ensuring your documents and data are kept safe and compliant with regulation. Services include: document storage and retrieval; secure data protection and media tape backup; secure confidential shredding and destruction services; scanning and imaging solutions; in-house file tracking solution for integration the practice management software; records management consultancy and policy advice.

Tel: 0870 908 8000

Email: enquiry@wincantonrm.co.uk

Website: www.wincantonrm.co.uk